CENTER
FOR
HERMENEUTICAL
STUDIES
in Hellenistic and Modern Culture

Graduate Theological Union & University of California-Berkeley

Berkeley, California

COLLOQUY
57

Associate Director: Kathleen M. Irwin

EXECUTIVE COMMITTEE of the Center for Hermeneutical Studies, 1988-89:

William S. Anderson	Professor of Classics, University of California, Berkeley
Michael Aune	Professor of Liturgics, Graduate Theological Union
Julian Boyd (Chairman)	Professor of English, University of California, Berkeley
James Jarrett	Professor of Education, University of California, Berkeley
Steven Knapp	Professor of English, University of California, Berkeley
Rebecca Lyman	Professor of Historical Theology, Graduate Theological Union
Mary E. Lyons	Professor of Homiletics, Graduate Theological Union
David Stagaman	Professor of Systematic Theology, Graduate Theological Union

The Center for Hermeneutical Studies arose as a response to a growing awareness of the fragmentation and lack of direction in humanistic research, specifically in the area of Hellenistic studies, post Biblical Judaica, and studies in early Christianity.

In the belief that (1) team effort is essential for real growth in these fields, and that (2) methodological breakthroughs will likely occur where scholars in a variety of fields encounter each other seriously in the pursuits of common interests, a group of New Testament scholars at the Graduate Theological Union in Berkeley formed the Center for Hermeneutical Studies during the Spring of 1969. The next step was the creation of a network of relationships and cooperation between scholars of the Graduate Theological Union and those in various fields within the University of California who share their interests in Hellenistic studies and in the problems of hermeneutics involved in their significance for modern culture.

The Center brings together faculty members of the departments of Classics, Comparative Literature, English, Folklore, History, Law, Near Eastern Studies, Rhetoric and others at the University of California, faculty from the Graduate Theological Union including the Center for Jewish Studies, as well as select graduate students from each institution, and from other universities and research institutes nearby.

CENTER
FOR
HERMENEUTICAL
STUDIES
in Hellenistic and Modern Culture

Graduate Theological Union & University of California-Berkeley

Berkeley, California

PROTOCOL OF THE FIFTY-SEVENTH COLLOQUY: 13 MARCH 1988

TEACHING AND LEARNING PRACTICE:

A RELATIONAL HERMENEUTIC FOR PROFESSIONAL SCHOOLING

David S. Steward
Professor of Religious Education
PACIFIC SCHOOL OF RELIGION
and
Rebecca Slough
GRADUATE THEOLOGICAL UNION

James Duke, editor

ISSN 0098-0900

Key Title:

Protocol of the colloquy of the Center for Hermeneutical Studies in Hellenistic and Modern Culture

Library of Congress Cataloging-in-Publication Data

Steward, David S.
    Teaching and learning practice : a relational hermeneutic for
professional schooling / David S. Steward and Rebecca Slough.
        p.   cm. -- (Protocol of the colloquy of the Center for
Hermeneutical Studies in Hellenistic and Modern Culture, ISSN
0098-0900 ; 57)
    ISBN 0-89242-058-8
    1. Theology--Study and teaching. 2. Theology--Study and teaching-
-Supervision. 3. Professional education.   I. Slough, Rebecca.
II. Title. III. Series: Colloquy (Center for Hermeneutical Studies
in Hellenistic and Modern Culture) ; 57.
BV4020.S74 1989
207'.1'1--dc20
                                                      89-7400
                                                        CIP

Published by

The CENTER FOR HERMENEUTICAL STUDIES
in Hellenistic and Modern Culture

2400 Ridge Road
Berkeley CA 94709 - USA

TABLE OF CONTENTS

TEACHING AND LEARNING PRACTICE: A RELATIONAL HERMENEUTIC FOR PROFESSIONAL SCHOOLING

David S. Steward and Rebecca Slough

INTRODUCTION

Professionals are those through whose action our society orients and frames, heals and reconciles itself and its members. Professionals bear witness to values; they embody an ethic; they seek to "make a difference that makes a difference" (Cf. Gregory Bateson, Mind and Nature: A Necessary Unity. N.Y.: Dutton, 1979) to those they serve.

Professional schools are schools like other schools. They rest on assumptions about how we teach and learn, and they are formed into institutions which reflect popular cultural values. In our culture there is a migration of cultural values accompanying the technical revolutions which have brought us mobility, affluence and an uncertain future. Professionals in our culture differ on which ethic they are to embody and the difference they are to make. How is practice to be understood, and taught? What agenda and institutional shape does professional schooling require these days?

This paper studies how the teaching and learning of professional practice is accomplished. It begins by considering how such a study should be conducted. First, it proposes action as the unit for study and suggests a multidisciplinary approach. Second, it identifies relationship as the element requiring special attention in the investigation. Third, it introduces the reflective process through which the teaching and learning of practice occurs.

Action As Unit

Most scholars approach their research on schooling with well developed methodological skills that reflect a single way to study the phenomenon. Recently scholars have come to see that the effort to order the world through a given methodology, while achieving powerful narrow band results, leaves many questions unaddressed.

Michael Cole illustrates a response to this problem in his studies of cognition and culture. (cf. M. Cole and S. Scribner, Culture and Thought. New York: Wiley, 1974, and "The zone of proximal development: where culture and cognition create each other," in Culture Communication and Cognition: Vygotskian Perspectives, ed. by James V. Wertsch. New York: Cambridge University Press, 1985). For Cole the problem comes not when one studies different cultures using models and methods of cognitive psychology. The problem comes when one attempts to interpret the differences among cultures which arise from such studies. Cole suggests that a division of labor that is dualistic often accompanies disciplinary research. He portrays such a division in the following table (p. 147).

Table 1. PSYCHOLOGY AND ANTHROPOLOGY: CONCEPTUAL POLARITIES

ANTHROPOLOGY	PSYCHOLOGY
Culture	Cognition
Higher functions	Elementary Functions
Products	Process
Content	Process
Group	Individual
Independent variable	Dependent variable
Observation	Experimentation
Field	Laboratory
Holistic	Analytic
Description	Explanation

Cole proposes an approach to the interpretation of cognition cross-culturally that begins with a different, wider band than either anthropology or psychology provides. He calls it "a sociocultural approach." The generation of an alternative to disciplinary theories brings with it a question: What is the unit of investigation through which the insights of several disciplinary theories can be tapped?

Cole identifies the unit for study as an individual engaged in goal-directed activity under conventionalized constraints. This unit is variously designated an "activity," a "task," an "event" (p. 158). These units are generally peopled by others, which means that "the acquisition of culturally appropriate behavior is a process of interaction...." (ibid). The work of sociocultural contextualists invites us to search for and use interactional units in a study of teaching and learning.

When activity is the unit of investigation, "the object is transformed into its subjective form or image. At the same time, activity is converted into objective results and products. Viewed from tnis perspective, activity emerges as a process of reciprocal transformations between the subject and object poles" (A.N. Leont'ev. "The problem of activity in psychology." In J. V. Wertsch. ed., The Concept Of Activity in Soviet Psychology. Armonk, N.Y.: Sharpe, 1981. Cf. Cole, p. 160). A static notion of the world waiting to be discovered does not match such a unit.

Chris Argyris (et al.) propose that "usable knowledge, in the context of social interaction" be studied. "This means, among other things, that the actor grasp what Lewin called the 'wholeness' of the problem." (Chris Argyris, Robert Putnam and Diana McLain Smith, Action Science. San Francisco: Jossey Bass, 1985, p. 42). Mainstream scientists, Argyris complains, seek precision, and therefore isolate fragments of social reality for study. His alternative, which he calls "action science," seeks high standards of rigor, but not precision in the mainstream sense. "...in action science we seek explanations that are optimally incomplete ...knowledge in the service of action should on the one hand include explanations that have gaps, and on the other hand should include ways of filling in the gaps in accordance with the purposes at hand" (p. 43). The purpose of action research is as much to "set problems" as to solve them.

"The theory of action approach," says Argyris, "begins with a conception of human beings as designers of action" (p. 80). "Designing action requires that agents construct a simpli-fied representation of the environment and a manageable set of causal theories that prescribe how to achieve the intended consequences" (p. 81). It is this process which action science observes. Beyond this, Argyris insists that action scientists are themselves designers.

Argyris calls his investigator an "interventionist." This is hardly a neutral role. If the sociocultural realm is understood only through activity (including language for which there must be a general social reference if it is to be understood), the design of action comes to be more important as a device to frame and control what is studied. It is as persons react to "environments" using their "causal theories" that the structure and meaning of what they do can become clear to them and to investigators.

Relationship as Context

Jerome Bruner asks a basic question which is at the heart of effective practice: "How does one know another mind?" (Actual Minds, Possible Worlds. Cambridge, Mass.: Harvard University Press, 1986). His answer: "through relationship."

Relationship, for Bruner, is a very physical, very social matter. His own research on infancy contributes to the documentation of a physiological capacity for relationship in mother-infant pairs. This natural predisposition to relate is called "attunement." It is now known that when the contacts are not possible, infants experience "failure to thrive," which may be fatal. When they occur, specific development of the neurological apparatus of the infant results. Infants are born to relate; when they do, they thrive and develop physiological capacities which extend their ability to process and interact with their environment.

These findings build on the pioneering research of Jean Piaget (Cf. The Origins of Intelligence in Children. New York: International Universities Press, 1952 1936). who conceptualized the capacity of the infant to relate, both to a social and physical world. That capacity has has been documented extensively through a myriad of physiological studies revealing a multitude of specific behaviors through which the link between an infant and a caregiver can be established. John Bowlby has documented the "attachment" between both animal and human mother and infant pairs, thereby contributing an evolutionary thrust to the research. (Cf. especially Attachment, Vol. I of Attachment and Loss. New York: Basic Books, 1969). Stanley Greenspan has done extensive clinical observation of infants with clinically referred parents. He views such infant and parent relationships to comprise a maladaptive environment, the consequences of which he has projected into the future development of the child (Stanley I. Greenspan, Intelligence and Adaptation. New York: International Universities Press, 1979).

Nelson Goodman, a philosopher, explored the nature of a social world which is being revised constantly by the activity of individuals. (Cf. especially Ways of Worldmaking. Indianapolis, Ind.: Hackett, 1978; and Of Mind and Other Matters. Cambridge, Mass.: Harvard University Press, 1984). Every person, he claims, is born into a world defined by conventions of language and culture. That world is the point of reference for each individual's values, beliefs and perceptions. Different persons are born into different worlds, but everyone is born into some world.

Every world is constructed, and each person, through living, builds out of her/his world and toward a new "version of world." Whereas "world" is the "given" into which a child is born, "version of world" is the construction the child makes. My "version" can, through negotiation with another person, bridge previously separate worlds and can, itself, become a world for someone else (e.g., one's children). The distinctively human activity in Goodman's world is construction from and of worlds. In this process one relies on the meanings already in place within the world. No one constructs new meanings except through these meanings.

Reflection Through Words

It is clear from the above that practice involves reflective thought. An understanding of how such thought works is essential for the teacher of practice.

Lev Vygotsky was a Russian psychologist who studied differences in how people thought. He was intrigued, for example, by a field study done by his friend, Luria, which showed that "for illiterate peasants, speech and reasoning simply echoed the patterns of practical, situational activity, while for people with some education the relation was reversed: abstract categories and word meanings dominated situational experience and restructured it" (Introduction by Alex Kozulin to Lev Vygotsky, Thought and Language. Cambridge, Mass.: The MIT Press, 1986 1934 , p. xl).

Vygotsky sought to explain such differences by a study of the roots and development of thought and speech. Since his concern was to discern the impact of each on communication, he needed to understand the relation between the two. But the methods of analysis employed by his predecessors either equated the two, or divided them into entirely different camps.

Vygotsky rejected the analytic method of his day which fragmented experience into "elements" that could be easily generalized, but which lost the character of the whole. (Cf. a chemical formula for water which "is equally applicable to the water in a great ocean and to the water in a raindrop" p. 4.) He proposed, instead, to study "units" which are "further unanalyzable and yet retain the properties of the whole" (p. 5). He turned to words, as distinct from thought or speech elements, and found his unit "in the internal aspect of the word, in word meaning" (p. 5).

Words are, of course, the instruments of both thought and speech. Their use reveals that both thought and speech are complex - functioning differently at different times for different people. The utterance of a word, by itself, does not insure communication. "Communication," says Vygotsky, "requires meaning - that is generalization - as much as signs. In order to convey one's experience or thought, it is imperative to refer them to some known class or group of phenomena" (p. 7).

Vygotsky studied both thought and speech and found an independently developing track for each. There is pre-linguistic thought and pre-intellectual speech. At a particular point thought and speech meet, at which point "thought becomes verbal, and speech rational" (p. 83).

The word is the key factor in the process of concept development toward which the meeting of thought and speech points, and through which communication occurs. Thought is the way a person is internally active. "Every thought tends to connect something with something else, to establish a relationship between things. Every thought moves, grows and develops, fulfills a function, solves a problem" (p. 218). The word (or any other sign) functions "as a means of focussing one's attention, selecting distinctive features and analyzing and synthesizing them" (p. 106). "Thought is not merely expressed in words; it comes into existence through them" (p. 218). Words come to be vehicles for thought.

But "the meaning of words are given ...in (a child's) conversations with adults" (p. 122). Children are not free to apply words just anywhere, if they are to communicate. Children do not "create (their) own speech, but acquire the speech of adults" (p. 122). It is the individual who brings the activity of thought, and the society which contributes the referent for speech. Together, through word meanings, they comprise a unity through which communication can happen within both self and society.

Reflection in Action

Professional practice involves action which takes place in relationship and in which reflection occurs.

Schoen has proposed a format for professional school teaching and learning in which reflection within the relationships between learner and teacher, and learner and world, are basic considerations. Schoen understands the professional to be a reflective practioner whose thought is not separated from practice, but whose reflective thought occupies a position within the practice itself. The result of this wholistic approach is a different kind of thinking - less rational and more reliant on the patterns of design and the arts. (The Reflective Practitioner. New York: Basic Books, 1982. See also, Chris Argyris and Donald A. Schoen, Theory in Practice: Increasing Professional Effectiveness. San Francisco: Jossey-Bass, 1974.) Schoen's more recent book, Educating the Reflective Practitioner (San Francisco: Jossey Bass, 1987), explores the teaching-learning process through which a person becomes a reflective practitioner. The heart of the process is a practicum. Here a teacher experienced in a professional practice "coaches" a student who is learning the same practice. The process rejects the assumption that one can know before one does (an assumption on which most schooling is predicated). Rather, one does before one knows, and learns through the artful critique and demonstration of the coach.

Schoen illustrates the way practitioners in architecture, engineering, music, and counseling design their practica. Within the practicum, both student and teacher engage in the practice of their profession. They also talk about what they are doing as they do it. It is through verbal interchange that reflection penetrates action and serves to refine it.

Two kinds of relationship can be derived from Schoen's format that are important in teaching and learning practice. The first is a supervisory relationship between an intern and an experienced practitioner. In this relationship, the supervisor practices the profession while teaching the intern. The music teacher plays; the architect designs - in response to the student's personal and professional needs. Through this process, the supervisor admits the intern into the profound and very personal struggles through which practice is shaped. It is this ability to reach out, invite in, accomplish personal sharing that makes the supervisory relationship basic to learning professional practice.

The second relationship supports the supervisory relationship, particularly in the development of useful professional concepts. This relationship is between a scholar/thinker who is outside the supervisory setting, and the members of the supervisory dyad. This is a consultation relationship through which the general concepts, refined by a scholarly discipline, are made available to facilitate reflection-in-action as it proceeds in the supervision relationship. Here the role of language in professional schooling becomes very clear.

Part of the task of professional schooling is to transmit the language of the community to the would-be professional. Part of the task is to help the student develop the ability to bring concepts to life by attaching them to a variety of activities in ways the community can recognize. Concept acquisition and concept use are verbal matters. Through language, activity and meaning are linked for a public.

The process of concept acquisition (the ability to collect a variety of cases under a single category which accurately reflects the experience of a community) is by no means easy. Nor is it ever completed. It is facilitated by the scholar/teacher using the dynamics of consultation.

It is the job of the scholar/teacher to know the concepts of a community, both historically and functionally. But the scholar/teacher must also facilitate the organization of conceptual material by the student intern in a way that is useful in the setting where professional work is to be done. The scholar/teacher, in this view, continues to organize concepts according to the methods of her/his discipline. But the presentation of those concepts is done for the sake of concept acquisition, in response to the "potential concepts" the intern and supervisor reveal as they struggle to talk about their work. The scholar/teacher introduces and develops concepts required for the community's health in response to the efforts made within the profoundly personal supervisory relationship to understand and talk about professional practice.

This paper explores these two relationships of professional schooling: the supervisory relationship between experienced practitioner and intern, and the consulting relationship between scholar/teacher and each member of the supervision dyad.

I. THE PROJECT

The "Theological Schools and Youth Ministries Project" (funded by a Lilly Foundation mini-grant, and by Pacific School of Religion) used a theory of action approach in its design and in the assumptions it made about the schooling event it studied. The analyses of data gathered through the project are multi-disciplinary. Each analysis was selected to reveal something about specific relationships to which the Project staff attended because they were believed to be significant in the teaching and learning of practice. The results of each analysis will be reported. The results will serve as a springboard to discuss the way each relationship is perceived to function in teaching and learning ministry. The discussion will suggest an hermeneutic for professional schooling where the teaching and learning of professional practice is at issue.

Network Center for the Study of Christian Ministry

The Network Center for the Study of Christian Ministry (NCSCM) is an alternative year of theological education supported by four schools in The Graduate Theological Union and delivered in the city of San Francisco. It seeks to impact both students and faculty from traditional seminaries by involving them in a "ministry-based" curriculum. Students commit themselves to an academic year of work, study and spiritual direction. City churches and service agencies are used as field sites. They are selected to reflect the range of human needs condensed in a city. At each site there is a skillful, Christian leader present to give supervision. Classes meet at the field sites and are taught by seminary faculty, joined whenever possible by front-line ministers as co-teachers. Bible, ethics, pastoral care, church administration, worship are standard fare. Each class is oriented to the structures and life of the city, and responds directly to the ministry settings from which students come. Each student is offered the resources of a spiritual director. There are retreats and planning sessions to help faculty, supervisors, spiritual directors and students become aware of one another.

The NCSCM has in place a structure for uncovering the needs of urban youth and for developing in seminarians both ideas about and experience in ministering to those needs. The structure is urban based, and centered in sites where ministry is practiced. It is organized less hierarchically than the seminary, has built-in accountability experiences from those served, and provides opportunity for extensive group process and the development of spiritual disciplines. It exists within the context of human needs and seeks to draw into itself resources from church, the academy and the Holy Spirit. It understands itself as contextual, dialogical and integrative. Whether and how these structures work to train persons to minister is what we are exploring.

It is within NCSCM that we have conducted our project. We have thought this to be appropriate because NCSCM bridges the gap between school and city; preparation and practice. In addition, NCSCM seeks to organize itself in terms of "called" Christian ministry; it serves people in crisis as well as through congregations; and it works actively for justice through a well-honed sense of preference for the poor. We studied two sites within NCSCM where the theological schooling focus was ministry with marginalized youth.

During the five years of its existence, NCSCM has begun to articulate its distinctive model for theological schooling. The basic terms of that model center on educational interchange framed by the forms of culture we know as Gospel and City. It is through these forms that God's love is revealed to us.

NCSCM affords an opportunity to explore how faculty, students and supervisors teach and learn to minister in settings which serve youth in crisis. NCSCM wishes to explore how classroom content, especially Bible and ethics, can be taught when ministry is the content to be learned, and especially the place of participation in ministry settings in that process. Its purpose is to demonstrate a model for teaching ministry which integrates the resources of seminary and church.

Project Design Elements

ASSUMPTIONS

Three questions reveal the scope of our interest. (1) Who are the people to whom those we train direct their ministry? (2) What counts as ministry to them? (3) What kind of schooling equips for ministry so understood? These questions served to frame the design of the project. Assumptions about youth (the client group), ministry and theological schooling are presented.

ASSUMPTIONS ABOUT YOUTH

Youth is both a new and a critical phenomenon in modern culture. Erik Erikson (cf. Identity, Youth and Crisis. New York: Norton, 1968) has brought youth into focus as a distinctive social phenomenon within the life cycle of an individual. The transitions between childhood and adulthood, family and the world of work, have become complex rites of passage involving peer cultures and a psycho-social moratorium. The tasks of youth (which Erikson catches up in the word, "identity") change with our changing world, making youth relative to the relativity of our times. It is out of such instability that the emergence of the next generation of adults takes place.

Stress, says Richard S. Lazarus and Susan Folkman (Stress Appraisal and Coping. New York: Springer, 1984), is an organizing concept which helps us understand a wide range of phenomena which are important in human adaptation. When stress is seen as a relationship which exceeds a youth's resources and endangers his or her well-being, its pervasiveness during times of transition becomes clear. Urban dwellers live in an unsettled and often violent environment. Changes in the adolescent (physical, emotional, cognitive, spiritual) interrupt those relationships which were stable before. Expansion of the world of the adolescent beyond the family contributes other interruptions. Stress becomes a mode of existence which characterizes the time of youth, and which cannot be overcome by manipulating specific life circumstances. Even when youth run away (e.g., from home) stress is not left behind, for the runaway cannot escape her/himself.

Martin E. P. Seligmann (Helplessness: on Depression, Development, and Death. San Francisco: W. H. Freeman, 1975) analyzes the negative results of stress. It is when persons are unable to control or predict in their worlds that helplessness sets in. Seligmann makes the stunning case that helplessness is learned; it, therefore, can be unlearned. Unlearning helplessness is much more difficult than learning it, but the task can be done.

Albert Bandura ("Self-efficacy." In Bandura, A., ed., Social Foundations of Thought and Action. Englewood Cliffs, NJ: Prentice Hall, 1986) shows that beliefs which persons have about their coping efficacy affect both emotional and behavioral reactions in stressful situations. Perceived self-efficacy is what is sought to overcome helplessness. The perception must, of course, be the youth's, and it develops through specific experiences of coping.

A healing response to stress needs to take into account the relationship of youth and environment (cf. Uri Bronfenbrenner, The Ecology of Human Development. Cambridge, Mass.: Harvard University Press, 1979). Emmy E. Werner and Ruth S. Smith (Vulnerable but Invincible: A Study of Resilient Children. San Francisco: McGraw-Hill, 1982) have followed multiracial children of poverty for 20 years, focussing on the factors involved in their ability to overcome stress. Both physical and social realms were carefully explored. They insist on the need for a transactional model of human development in which the interconnections within the wider social world are included in the assessment of a youth's immediate social environment.

Key assumptions related to youth are that they experience transition, stress, inability to predict or control, little perceived self-efficacy, relationship with environ-environment.

Not surprisingly, we have already discerned that urban youth with whom NCSCM work are characterized by transition and stress. There are limits (sometimes severe) to their ability to control and their ability to predict. They often lack a caring environment and strength of belief in themselves. These circumstances are linked to the stresses of the San Francisco urban context, the fact the San Francisco youth are frequently required to take care of themselves in out-of-stage ways, and the presence in San Francisco of a wide array of confusing psycho-sexual options.

ASSUMPTIONS ABOUT MINISTRY

James Earl Breech (The Silence of Jesus. Philadelphia: Fortress Press, 1983, and 1986 E.T. Earl Lectures, Pacific School of Religion) argues that Jesus's ministry, like his parables and sayings, is distinctive because it does not provide an ending which gives typical answers or morals to the hearer. Instead, Jesus invites his hearers to be active "in story," making their way responsively through the various interruptions which life provides, while not forsaking their "call." Ministry is response in this world according to the terms of one's call.

Jon Sobrino (The True Church and the Poor. New York: Maryknoll, 1984) argues Jesus's "preference for the poor." Herein he finds the content of "call," and therefore of ministry. Poverty, he suggests, is a much more dynamic concept than can be caught up in dollar earnings. Poverty is a state of lost dignity. Liberation is into the dignity of full humanness. It is an enpowerment to live expectantly into a future. This is what drives Christian ministry. To restore dignity is a social as well as a psychological matter. It requires political as well as intellectual involvement.

Henri J. M. Nouwen has for fifteen years written about ministry from the point of view of the one who ministers. It is who the minister is, as well as what the minister does, which reveals the focus and power of the Gospel. Ministry happens when, beyond skills of ministering, life experience is given by the minister (cf. Creative ministry. Garden City, N.J.: Doubleday, 1971) and received from those to whom the ministry is addressed, with thanks (Gracias: A Latin American Journal. San Francisco: Harper and Row, 1983).

Key assumptions related to ministry are that ministry involves living in story, liberation into dignity, empowering living, giving ourselves and receiving the selves of others.

ASSUMPTIONS ABOUT THEOLOGICAL SCHOOLING

There is considerable criticism these days about schooling in general, and about theological schooling in particular. Seymour B. Sarason (Schooling in America. New York: The Free Press, 1983) argues that all American schools are in trouble because we assume that education best takes place in schools. From this assumption there appears the double gap between schools and world on the one hand, and between preparation and practice on the other.

Schooling, says Henry A. Giroux (Theory and Resistance in Education: A Pedagogy for the Opposition. South Hadley, Mass.: Bergin & Garvey, 1983) takes place in institutions which serve particular, ideological interests. This claim does not exclude the theological seminary, which is structured to serve the interests of the academy and the church. Serving particular interests is not, in itself, unworthy, unless that service preempts other loyalties. It is when loyalty to the church or academy is left unchecked by other loyalties, that it becomes oppressive. Resistance takes the form of challenging the right of an ideologically driven institution to control the individual. Resistance can be developed conceptually by insisting that there is "a universe of alternatives" to present schooling practice (cf. Seymour B. Sarason, The Culture of the School and the Problem of Change. 2nd ed. Boston: Allyn and Bacon, 1982). Resistance can be developed on humanistic grounds by rejecting those forms of schooling which perpetuate themselves by arguing that oppositional behavior is deviant rather than rooted in moral and political indignation (cf. Henry A. Giroux. "Theories of Reproduction and Resistance in the New Sociology of Education: a Critical Analysis," The Harvard Educational Review. VOL. 53, No. 3, August 1983, pp. 257-293). Resistance can be developed on theological grounds by maintaining the essential mystery of the Gospel in tension with the mandate to be active in a world which cries for liberation (cf. Segundo, The Community Called Church. New York: Maryknoll, 1973).

Alice Frazier Evans, Robert A. Evans and William Bean Kennedy, (Pedagogies for the Non-poor. Orbis, 1987) promote "transformative education:" education to raise consciousness and to produce action to change oppressive structures. They seek to root their definitions descriptively, making the non-poor "those with low infant mortality rates and high life expectancy, those above the poverty line, or, more simply, those who are well fed." They assert that such folk are ideological captives to the North American "middle class cocoon" and they wish to excise them from it. Transformative education comes through four steps: new consciousness, lifestyle change, political/social action, and conversion. It requires commitment of time and energy, radical change of environment, risk-taking, community of support, reflection and "data" from outside. These steps and requirements are consistent with Marxist and liberation based prescriptions for educational process.

Edward B. Farley, (Theologia: The Fragmentation and Unity of Theological Education. Philadelphia: Fortress Press, 1983) argues that theological schools have become fragmented both in their vision and in their curriculum. The specialties of scientific organization have come to be the model for theological curriculum, with the result that human wholeness has been lost in the shuffle. Charles M. Wood (Vision and Discernment: An Orientation in Theological Study. Atlanta, Ga.: Scholars Press, 1985) proposes an integrated view of theological education "as the enterprise of developing a capacity and disposition for theological inquiry" (p. vii). He believes that "one learns to make judgments chiefly by making judgments, and then examining their grounds and implications, reflecting on one's performance, and trying again," (p. 81) and that this should be reflected in the structure of theological schooling.

Joseph C. Hough, Jr. and John B. Cobb, Jr. (Christian Identity and Theological Education, Chico, Calif.: Scholar's Press, 1985) focus, in their study of theological schooling, on the church as the context within which Christians live. They sketch the structure of that context, insisting that it encompass both history and the world as Christian and non-Christian persons have seen it. Then they propose descriptors to reflect its essential nature, which they discern in its practice. The church is they assert, when the church sees itself as a human, caring, evangelistic community for the world, the oppressed, all peoples, women. Such a community functions as it integrates divisions in the world through repentence, response and worship. Professional leadership in this kind of church requires a "practical Christian thinker," one for whom reflection and action are part of the same process.

Key assumptions related to theological schooling are that it struggles with the isolation of schooling from culture, the relation of theological schooling to ideologies, and inquiry and social context as points of integration for theological schooling.

THE SITES

Within NCSCM two sites were selected for our work, based on their ministry to marginalized youth.

One site is a church which serves a variety of street people and transients, as well as recent immigrants from South America. Its tutoring center serves about 50 youth and their families, 50% of whom are Hispanic, 25% Black and the rest other ethnic groups, with a noticeable presence of Native Americans. Youth are tutored in basics and English as a second language. Staff link with the schools, and counsel with families.

Across the street from the church is a notoriously violent, mostly Black housing project. The church draws from this area and has begun Sunday School, after school and Saturday "cultural enrichment" programs for preteens and early teens from the neighborhood. Currently about 10 youth participate in this congregationally based activity.

The second site is a private agency in San Francisco which deals with homeless, runaway and throwaway youth, 60% of whom are white, and 40% of whom are Black, Hispanic or Asian. 1200 youth between 13 and 18 are served each year on the street, and about 350 come to the Center itself. The Center provides a wide variety of counseling and referral services, medical aid, some food and second hand clothing, tutoring, and interpretation (both political and theological) to churches and other city agencies. The main task of the Center is to divert youth from the street through family counselling and reunification, foster care, and independent living. The program includes night street workers who minister to young male hustlers. Drug and alcohol abuse are major problems.

THE TEAM

A team of six persons from NCSCM was involved in the study: two site supervisors, two site interns and two faculty members. The selection of the team was largely site driven, though the outcome has been the gathering of six quite distinctive "worlds."

THE CLASS

During the time of this study, a small research class was convened to participate in the conceptualization and pursuit of the research program. The class did background reading, discussed issues of theory and design, and participated in interviewing team members.

THE PROCESS

The process was an inductive one. We asked team members to "attend" to their work, and to "format" it, using a log protocol we designed. We asked faculty members and supervisors to write one log each week reflecting experiences important to their roles. Interns were asked to write three logs each week: one each on their experience in class, in supervision, and in ministry assignments. The team met monthly to discuss and to extend the logs. Three of the meetings were half day meetings during which the team could do more intensive work together. During the last half of the project, three monthly interviews were held with each team member, to extend and focus their log reflections.

The project director duplicated logs and circulated them to all team members. He also wrote feedback to team members on each log submitted. The content of the feedback included comments on log structure, and reflection on the issues raised in the logs.

The Instruments

LOGS

A log protocol was developed to provide a grammar for reporting experience. The grammar reflects an action-reflection-action model, designed to encourage reporting of role appropriate experience. There are five steps to the protocol. The first step, Focus, is a request for log writers to state the role appropriate action about which they want to write. The second step, Concern, is a request for them to state why the focussing act is important to them. The third step, Illustration, asks for a description of the event which illustrates the action they have selected. The fourth step, Learning, asks for reflection growing from the illustration, about themselves, about those they served, and about their role. The fifth step, Decision, asks for a follow up action, based on what they have learned.

The log protocols were modified mid-year, in the light of a preliminary analysis of the way logs were being written, to acknowledge that response rather than initiation is the first step in thinking about an experience. The revised logs begin with Goals brought by log writers to their roles. The second step is to state an Activity they did to pursue their goal. The third step is to <u>Report</u> what happened when they did their activity. The fourth step is to reflect on their <u>Learning</u>. The final step is to <u>Evaluate</u> what needs to change the next time through.

During the 14 weeks of the Fall Semester, one faculty member turned in 15 logs; the other 12 logs. One supervisor turned in 14 logs; the other 6 logs. One intern turned in 25 logs; the other 15 logs. (Interns had been requested to turn in 3 logs per week for an anticipated total of 42 logs each).

For Spring Semester we asked for 9 weeks of logging plus three interviews. Both faculty members turned in 9 logs. One supervisor turned in 9 logs; the other 7 logs. One intern turned in 25 logs (of 27 requested); the other 12 logs.

FEEDBACK

Written responses were given whenever a set of logs was turned in. Since logs were not always submitted on a regular basis, and in fact have often arrived in "batches," feedback responses were returned on only 22 occasions. However, every log was taken into account in the feedback.

During Fall Semester, feedback included two kinds of responses: instructions for refining logging skills and commentary on the issues and ideas which surfaced. Each feedback also included efforts to support the person in the difficult task of logging. Fall semester feedback totaled 95 pages.

At the end of Fall Semester, we considered carefully the structural role played by the feedback. We understood the recursive nature of the logging exercise. The action-reflection-action loop, we came to see, was interrupted by the feedback. This made us think more carefully about the log-feedback loop, and to note the assymetry between tight log structure and loose feedback structure. We revised Spring Semester logging, and included interview sessions, in part to balance the formats for expression by team members on the one hand and by project director on the other. During Spring Semester, feedback included no reference to logging skills. It spoke to issues raised in the logs - seeking to make explicit and flesh out what the log writer said, and to continue giving support for writing the logs. Forty six and a half pages of feedback were returned.

INTERVIEWS

During the Spring Semester, three interviews were conducted with each team member, to explore and flesh out what appeared in the logs. The March 10 interviews focussed, generally, on the understanding each team member had of their role (intern, supervisor, teacher). The April 14 interviews focussed on progress made during the year in role, including progress made by the team partners for whom one was role responsible. The May 11 interviews focussed on an evaluation of the year's experience and advice for theological schooling.

Interviewers prepared by reading the logs written by those interviewed. Questions were framed using the content of those logs. They focused on recent logs giving team members a chance to elaborate beyond the structure imposed by the logs. When necessary, material from earlier logs was introduced, usually for comparative purposes. The exploration of feelings and relationships was prominent in the interviews, and the conceptual constructions team members derived from their NCSCM experience. In the interviews, team members were invited to "help us understand" what they experienced and thoughtabout their alternative theological schooling. Interviews were conducted by members of an advanced research class which read and discussed around the project during the year. Each interview took about one half hour, was recorded and transcribed.

OTHER DOCUMENTS

Two other kinds of documentation have been collected: Adjective Check Lists and autobiographies.

The Adjective Check List (ACL) is a standardized instrument designed to reveal how a person perceives someone. It is comprised of 300 adjectives which can be checked selectively. The data can be ordered on 37 different scales. We asked each team member to complete the ACL on "self," "ideal minister to youth you serve," and "youth you serve." This was done in September, February, and May. The ACL lets us look for stability and change of perception over time.

During the first half day team meeting, each person gave an autobiographical presentation. These were transcribed and were analyzed for methaphoric content.

II. THE ANALYSES

Our exploration of teaching and learning practice begins with a description of the nature and shape of the supervision relationship, as participants see it. That framework invites specific probes into participants' perceptions of self and role during their experience of supervision, and their thinking about ministry - the practice with which they are dealing. The final analysis deals with a meta-relationship through which each participant is kept aware of the concepts and reflective process involved in practice.

The interviews provided the material to describe the perception supervisors and interns had of supervision, and of their experience of it during the year. These descriptions have been collated into descriptions of each supervisor-intern dyad. The points (and much of the language) of the descriptions are from the interviews, making the renderings interesting as artifacts from self-report (as distinct from theoretical constructions). Every effort was made, working from interview transcripts, to include every point advanced. The coherence of each dyadic report comes from the interviews and may reflect, though we are unable to demonstrate this, the impact of year long log reflection.

The Adjective Check List gave us the perceptions team members held about themselves and the roles with which they were involved in ministry practice. By taking repeated measures, we were able to construct a flow chart on the instrument's Need Scales for each team member. We could, then, compare not only the perception of team members with that of the general population, but also their reported "flow of needs" with the memory reported in the interviews.

The language which team members used in their autobiographies, logs and interviews was examined to uncover metaphors employed to organize thinking about ministry. Continuities and shifts in these usages were compared with the flow of interview self-report data.

A fourth analysis was done on log feedback, using speech act theory. This was our effort to explore the consultation relationship through which team members were trained to do log reflection. The initial tasks of the log feedback was to refine participants' skill in log logic and writing. We came to believe that the feedback also supported the supervision relationship by acknowledging the work that was done there. Over the year, log feedback came to emphasize concepts latent or explicit in the logs which the log feedback writer found to be important to the supervision relationship or to the ministry to which that relationship referred. The analysis of log feedback sought to uncover speech patterns that might indicate how a consultant helps or hinders the development of concepts which relate to practice.

Each of the four analyses (of supervision using a self-report method; of personal and role perception using a standardized instrument; of conceptual organization using a metaphor technique; of feedback using a speech act method) reveals limited information about the supervision and consultation relationships studied here. This information will be reported. Then we will discuss implications for teaching and learning practice which we have derived from these pattern fragments.

The Nature and Shape of Supervision:
a description of two supervision dyads
gleaned from interviews

Data for the Interview Analysis comes from three half hour interviews conducted with each team member a month apart during the last half of the project. During each interview questions were asked about the experience and role relationships of the team member. Transcriptions of the interviews of interns and supervisors were read to uncover what was said about the structure and the process of supervision. Two very different supervision strategies will be described, one for each supervisor-intern dyad. The first dyad is the supervisor and intern from the church near the housing project. The second dyad is the supervisor and intern from the private agency dealing with street youth.

THE FIRST DYAD

Supervision, affirmed Supervisor One (S-1), requires awareness of one's own growing edges, willingness to prepare for each session, and the ability to craft clear learning goals. Lest these be seen to be mechanical factors, S-1 went on to label the process of supervision "a wilderness experience" for both parties. Nothing about supervision is neat and tidy, safe and sane.

For S-1 supervision is rooted in relationship. The supervisor brings to the relationship an ability to focus keen attention on the intern. Preparation for a session involved gathering himself emotionally, intellectually and spiritually, away from the demands of the parish and toward the experiences of the intern. The heart of supervision rests not in tasks assigned by the church to the intern, but in the person of the intern.

The supervisor also brings an ability to format the supervision hour into a learning experience. He looks at the situation the intern has brought to the session and works to surface the feelings involved. He tries to analyze and define the structure of the situation, using his own repertoire of past experience. He affirms the intern in ways indicated by the feelings the intern brings as well as by the performance reported.

S-1's intern (I-1) reported a remarkably similar view of supervision. In his experience, the supervisor listened, clarified, affirmed. His supervisor made his needs the basis of their relationship. Supervision, they agreed, involves "making needs visible" to both partners, but especially to the intern. This is primarily an interpersonal rather than a conceptual task.

* * * * *

How did S-1 and I-1 understand their supervision relationship to develop? "You can't supervise until each person sees how the other is a resource." said S-1. I-1 responded in kind: "peerage breeds intimacy."

S-1 confessed the "pull" of task responsibilities early in the supervision relationship. The church hired the intern to get certain things done. The standing of both supervisor and intern with the congregation depended, in part, on performance of those tasks. S-1 expressed some early frustration about using the supervision hour to establish their relationship rather than to make and check job assignments. I-1 agreed. He, too, felt the weight of task expectations. "I began with a role perception from the congregation," he said. For both S-1 and I-1, the first major task in supervision was to reframe their task. In the words of S-1, they had to get "from goals to covenant." The establishment of covenant became the first and year-long task of supervision, from which both job organization and personal support flowed.

Supervision, affirmed I-1, "helps shift my perspective" from me as intern-minister over/against the congregation to me as intern-minister in relation to each member of the congregation. This gets done through "a dialogue of difference." The dialogue required the intern "to reach out and touch" his clients so as to "empower them."

S-1 agreed. Personal difference is at the heart of supervision. The supervisor's first task, said S-1, was "to discover what I had to give." This involved attending specifically to the situation and experiences of I-1. "I tried to emphasize to I-1 how he was different. I did this so he could come to see himself clearly and to help him overcome stereotypical thinking about others." I-1 responded. He offered fewer "answers" and more acknowledgements of his "perspective."

Supervision operates through a covenant, said S-1, which is the result of a movement from "no relation to a trust relation." The trust relation is of two types. First, the intern must come to trust himself. Second, the intern and the supervisor must come to trust one another. These two trust relations are the agenda and fruit of supervision.

The trick, said S-1, is to use what you know to "generate personal openness." This requires a lot of personal preparation on the part of the supervisor. S-1 found it necessary to spend an hour before the supervision session to think, reflect, pray his way into the session itself. He found the logging exercise to be valuable. Since both S-1 and I-1 shared logs, these helped the focussing process over time.

S-1 knew how different I-1 was from him. He knew how important it was to let I-1 be active in revealing himself. At the same time, S-1 was skilled in discerning the feelings of I-1 and knew that feelings can be shared across different life experiences. S-1 believed that the development and maintenance of a covenant relationship required him to evoke the world and values of I-1. But these are tender matters that require trust to share. I-1 told how S-1 did it. "S-1 talks of his feelings when they are what both of us are feeling." I-1 found this to be an invitation for him to minister to S-1. When I-1 tried to do this, he found himself addressing the feeling in his own life. I-1 advanced in his self-understanding through such collegial sharing. Important learning happened in the process of pastoring the supervisor.

A ministry setting to marginalized persons can result in the experience of fear and failure on the part of the intern. This happened to I-1. Therapy for this result was provided by the personal sharing of S-1 and I-1. "Alignment" is what S-1 called it: the willingness to confess vulnerability to one another and to be open to expressions of feeling.

Sharing feelings is not the ultimate goal of ministry. Such sharing, however, acknowledged the emotional lens through which their reflections passed and through which their responses to the congregation were constructed. I-1 designated a next step in the supervision process as "to get beyond feelings to reasons and the realistic."

Goals, said S-1, are set in and from the ministry context. It is these goals, not the expectations from role or congregation, that supervisor and intern must address. S-1 and I-1 came to understand "the ministry context" to include their own perceptions and feelings. I-1 learned as he experienced the way S-1 listened to his differences that he had to listen to the differences represented in his clients. He discerned that all of them shared feelings of failure and pain. I-1 then reported learning two things. First, he had been projecting his own feelings of failure and pain onto the youth he served, seeking thereby to relieve himself from those feelings. This permitted him to tell his clients what to do from a safe emotional distance. S-1's expressions of vulnerability in the supervision session helped him see that his defensive maneuver had its limits. Second, he learned how vital it is to learn the language of the marginalized. English has many dialects; the same word can mean different things, and some words seldom used in the church have powerful meanings on the street. To use church-talk on the street would be to distance himself from those he served.

I-1 found it necessary to reframe his understanding of the youth he served. He sought to construct a context for ministry where he acted as a brother toward the youth. He began saying "my brothers and sisters," not "them." He came to a great discovery. This shift was accomplished, not by a deeper look at the youth, but "by looking at myself."

For both S-1 and I-1, supervision became a covenant relationship (replacing role and congregational expectations) and dealt with a ministry context peopled by brothers and sisters (rather than the variety of "thems" which I-1 was expecting to serve). These reframings came at a price. They remained tenuous at best for both parties. Throughout the process of supervision S-1 practiced a strategy of hope. In a ministry to the marginalized, he said, there must be "high tolerance for change, ambiguity, failure." But in the face of these realities, the minister must know that life is still good and that persons are to be esteemed. This perspective carried over into supervision.

"Encouragement." This followed feelings and realism as I-1's summary of what supervision with S-1 gave him. S-1 worked hard to discern the practical impact of I-1's background and manner on their supervision relationship and on I-1's ministry. He shared with, clarified, and pressed I-1 "in the light of his strength." His purpose was to "show esteem by paying attention." I-1 found that receiving affirmation in supervision strengthened his ability to affirm his clients. This process was important in the entire year's work.

Following a time, when I-1 experienced abandonment by his youth and a deep sense of personal failure, S-1 structured a month of supervision sessions around "the gifts we bring" and "the gifts our people bring." This challenge to the label of "badness" I-1 had placed on his youth and on himself turned things around. Subsequently, I-1 reported an event and a learning. The event was his effort to walk the streets, despite considerable dread, to find the youth who had left his program. When he did, they hugged him. He experienced a totally unexpected ecstasy and renewal. His learning was that affirmation must extend beyond what others give; it must involve his own ability to affirm. S-1 required I-1 to identify his own gifts during supervision, and I-1 used that approach with his youth as the year proceeded.

S-1 and I-1 reported a supervision experience rooted in a covenant relationship and centered around a personalized ministry context in which hope framed fear and failure. Tasks of congregational life were framed by these realities, making them invitations for listening, clarifying and affirming even beyond the supervision session.

THE SECOND DYAD

Supervisor Two (S-2) understood the personal, relational framework given to supervision by S-1. "A good supervisor is somebody who has time and can focus on where your intern is at and be aware of the issues they're going through." But S-2 did not find that comfortable or appropriate to his context. "This kind of other-oriented stuff doesn't apply to me," he said. S-2 revealed a supervisorial style that is clearly alternative to the one pursued by S-1.

From the beginning, S-2 found himself too busy and too politically vulnerable to develop a personal supervisorial relationship with his Intern (I-2). In the initial interview, S-2 found the applicant "a very nice person--very sincere," but he was uncertain about her ability "to contribute to staff efforts and work with the kids." He hired her because "either you take her or you don't get anybody." He assumed it would be "a great learning experience for her."

For S-2 the initiative for structuring the supervision session rested with the intern. It is interns who must "bring an understanding of what they need to get out of it." The supervisor "facilitates" - serves as "a sounding board." It is "the environment itself," not the supervision process, that makes the experience of supervision good. Although head of an institution which serves street youth, S-2 does not relate on a regular basis with the youth. He is distant from "the environment itself." And, he makes clear, a person does not come to this site to get emotionally or spiritually "fed."

S-2 identified two reality elements to support his position. First, he sees his position at the head of an institution in political terms. "At work you've got to be very careful because you can get nailed to the wall very fast." Because the intern is a member of the staff, it is not possible to involve her in special confidences. Roles must be kept clear. Second, S-2 is aware of the power of language to distort meaning. "As soon as you take something out of individual experience and try to communicate to somebody else, you lose the translation, just by definition." A struggle to share and learn through language is a high-risk affair.

* * * * *

What kind of supervisorial relationship developed between S-2 and I-2? At the beginning, S-2 turned I-2 loose to get used to the city street environment and to craft a role in which she could be comfortable. "It's real different from a church environment. It's not just like working in the city, but working in the shit hole." S-2 told her: "We're going to throw you into the drop-in area and you'll get supervision in terms of that stuff. I'll be around to talk to you about theological or conceptual things, but basically you're just going to be a regular staff person for two or three days a week. Good luck."

From afar, S-2 perceived I-2 to adapt and perform well. In contrast, I-2 reported frustration. She was dropped into an alien environment and had to rely on the role definitions she had learned in a suburban church. "Ministry," she affirmed, "is to be able to answer what is the meaning of life questions." This verbal, authoritarian role was not easy to translate into street ministry. Early on, fellow staff members warned her against using "spiritual language." But when she experimented with street language (called a situation "shitty"), the youth expressed shock that a minister would do so.

I-2 centered on language and answers. She looked hard for places to deliver these core expressions of ministry. Supervision sessions were not entirely satisfactory at the beginning. "We were never alone together," she complained of her supervision sessions. Meetings were irregular, and when they occurred, they were held in an office open to overhearing and interruption. The sessions were usually conducted late Friday afternoon - the last weary business of the week. "In all the hubbub we missed relationship."

A dance began between I-2 and S-2 around the proper content for supervision sessions. S-2 declined to structure the sessions, remembering the "laid back" way his urban supervisor had worked. I-2 personalized the experience. "When I get in supervision I usually don't think about the kids. I think about S-2's needs. I'm there to support S-2. I think prayer does that. When he knows I'm praying for him he knows I'm supporting him."

But S-2 was not responsive. "She would pray and I would sit there and let her do it," he said. "She wanted me to talk about my own personal experience of faith. I don't do that as a rule. I don't self-disclose. I am in a specific role and for her to know (too much about my agenda or thinking is inappropriate). I can share information. I can share experience. I can give my own staff advice. But there's a line that I'm not going to cross, and it would get her upset because she wanted more from me than I felt comfortable giving her."

I-2 captured the outcome of the dance. "When I'm in control it's exciting for me." Both S-2 and I-2 maintained a supervision relationship in which each insisted on a "language game" which would keep them in control. Since S-2 felt responsibility in supervision only to answer questions I-2 raised, he did not have to challenge her effort to control directly. He only had to defend himself. The location and irregularity of supervision helped him do this. In the absence of challenge, I-2 settled into her "answer man" understanding of ministry and sharpened it, using S-2's behavior as a pattern. The best experiences of ministry, she reported, occur when "I feel needed. They ask the questions that I've been trained to answer."

In the final analysis, pain and loneliness which I-2 experienced in the work site and on the streets could not be dealt with in supervision. "I've had a relatively painless life," I-2 said. "But when you walk in everyday and you see pain, you have to put up defenses against it. I find myself trying not to be involved. Right now I'm trying to disassociate myself at work." I-2 came to be very pessimistic about urban street ministry. "As a pastor of a congregation, one represents a community of faith. But on the street, I feel I'm alone. I'm I-2 the Christian...not really backed by a community. I have not bothered to use the resources of the church community." As a result, I-2 backed away from the street. "I went in with the idea that I minister to the kids. In reality I (have come to) minister to the staff. The kids come and go, (but) the relationship with the staff is everyday (and they can validate you").

Toward the end of the year, S-2 organized supervision around articulating the theological nature of the church in the city. This was the last straw for I-2. She had offered herself as a listening ear for his personal faith needs. S-2 responded with an intellectual formulation. She found this response to be an "attack" rather than an "encouragement." "We don't share personally," she said. "I share personally. He shares institutionally." One day she wrote an "angry log" which presented her version of the church for the city. It was a needed response, she said, because "S-2 sets the agenda when we go in (the supervision session) and what we talk about. Our perspectives on the church are very different. I felt the need to be specific and clear about my view. Lots of time I didn't feel that S-2 was listening, because there was not dialogue. I don't think we've done street theology. I think street theology is an emotional, personal issue. For him it's institutional - administrative. We're operating out of totally different planes of ministry, so that it's hard to be in dialogue. We don't want to switch places. (What S-2 gave me) I knew already. It's not a new learning process."

By the end of the year, I-2 had been able to resolve many of her tensions. Staff persons had come to talk with her about personal problems in areas she felt she was a ministerial expert. Supervision sessions had become less intense. "S-2 likes to talk and I enjoy listening so that's kinda how it's gone. My freedom is not talking, and I'm great at manipulating it so he talks. I didn't look for supervision. His confusion over what supervision should be and my confusion over what I expect from him is OK. We've made our own space in that relationship. We call it supervision or we can just call it a time together." In the end, street youth are not mentioned. "I'll go back into the parish."

Perceptions of Self and Roles:
patterns revealed by a standardized instrument.

The Adjective Check List (ACL) consists of 300 adjectives and adjectival phrases commonly used to describe a person's attributes. It may be administered to an individual to elicit a self-evaluation or a characterization of someone else..." (Harrison G. Gough, and Alfred B. Heilbrun, Jr., The Adjective Check List Manual, 1980 Edition, Palo Alto, Ca.: Consulting Psychologists Press, 1980, publisher's introduction).

We have used the ACL to give us an independent measure of the perception team members have of themselves, minister to youth, and youth they serve. Each team member was asked to complete an ACL covering each category at the beginning, in the middle, and at the end of the project. This produced a total of 9 ACLs completed by each team member. We have scored each ACL and have derived scale scores on the number of favorable and unfavorable adjectives checked, to get an overall impression of team members' perception; and on 14 Need Scales, to get a more detailed view of team members' perception of each person/role tested.

Our data permits us to give a profile of the perception each team member has of self, minister and youth at three points in time during the year. The profile is comprised from the scale scores, but requires some clinical judgment to interpret. The Scoring Manual supplies various ways of talking about each scale. We have selected or adapted choices within the Manual which we believe represent the context of our study fairly. (Appendix 1 presents the interpretive wording we have given to each scale score.)

The ACL reveals perceptions a person has of self or other. Such perceptions tend to be conservative over time. The conservative nature of the instrument is increased when it is administered to check someone's perception of the same person several times. Therefore shifts in score are especially interesting. We have recorded all scale scores that exceed one standard deviation from the normal population, and have used descriptors from these scales to present the perceptions our team members gave of self, minister and youth. (See Appendix 2) The profiles we give in the analysis below are descriptions of how the person scored is perceived to be different from the normal population. Shifts detailed deal with these "noticeable" differences.

Perception of self results are presented first, under the assumption that these will be the most stable. Perception of the role of minister and of youth have some personal distance from the reporter. Whether and how they differ from perception of self will be of interest.

THE FIRST DYAD

At the beginning of the project, Supervisor One (S-1) perceived his social attributes to make him special (noticeably different from the norm). More than most, he believed, he needed to relate to others, to help them and to take them into account. He described himself as an outgoing person.

This profile remained constant throughout the year. The winter profile added a need to avoid risk. This is not surprising given the personal expenditure required of S-1 during the fall in dealing with the AIDs death of several of his parishoners. By springtime, the tentativeness had gone and was replaced by a set of powerful self affirming attributes: the need to be in charge, to reflect, to do well, to get his due. It is clear that by the end of the year S-1 saw himself in a different, more actively balanced way. Not only did he care for others; he also cared for his own efficacy in what he did.

At the beginning of the project S-1 perceived the role, minister to youth, in terms very much like he perceived himself. Such a minister needed to relate to others and to help others. Such a person would be outgoing. But it was clear to S-1 that a minister to youth could expect to face some interpersonal challenges. Such a person also needed to be in charge, to get others' attention and ought not to be easily flapped. It is interesting to note the extent to which this profile of minister to youth forecasts S-1's final self profile.

By wintertime, S-1 found it difficult to make the role, minister to youth, exceptional. Both relational and self affirming attributes had dropped out. Now such ministers were perceived to go beyond the norm only in endurance (needing to do their job) and they ought not to be easily flapped. During this season S-1 definitely did not find ministry to be easy.

The spring profile saw S-1 return to the perception he had in the fall. Ministers to youth need to relate to others, to be in charge and to help others. The added attributes in spring carry much of the self affirming character of his spring view of self: need to do well, to do the job, to get their due, to be unbothered by self doubt.

At the beginning of the project, S-1 perceived the youth he served to diverge sharply from the norm on 12 of the 14 need scales. He perceived in them needs for emotional support, needs to assert themselves and make themselves visible, needs to be in perpetual motion. The needs themselves may not be unusual for adolescents. What make S-1's profile striking is the extreme to which he saw these needs expressed by the youth. Four of the scales reached the unusual level of statistical significance: the need to cope with stress, to be easily distracted/redirected, to be wary of close ties with others, and to get quick gratification. The disturbing excess is reflected in S-1's general descriptors (both of which reach strong statistical significance): he perceived these youth as self deprecating and pessimistic about the future.

S-1 maintained his perception of these youth with great tenacity during the year. The winter profile records the same 12 scale scores, and the spring profile records 11 of the same 12. The only change is a modest movement on most items toward the norm. Now only one of the general descriptors carries statistical significance (pessimistic about the future).

S-1 contributed profiles on himself and the role of minister to youth which shifted in interesting ways during the year. All these profiles maintained an interpersonal core (with the exception of the dark winter minister profile). Both self and minister profiles reveal the impact of severe winter job stress. The minister profile seems to forecast the final self profile. All of this activity occurred while virtually no change was reported in S-1's perception of youth. We take this to indicate that S-1's world was interpersonally charged and that S-1 was not so active "in the world" as he was in person-to-person interchange. This pattern matches S-1's sacramental style of ministry, and his clinical style of supervision.

At the beginning of the project, Intern One (I-1) perceived himself to need to be in charge and to relate to others. This reflects the same self and ministry balance to which S-1 came: a focus on relationship and a focus on self affirmation. The stress of the placement - the difficulty of the youth work and the personal tragedies in the parish - were reflected in the winter profile. I-1 continued to see himself as needing to be in charge, but he dropped the needs to relate and added the need to get his due.

By springtime, both winter items had retreated to the normal range. The need to relate to others had returned and he had added the need to do his job and to help others. Generally, he saw himself as not easily flapped.

In the fall, I-1 had a long laundry list of attributes for minister with youth. His list included virtually all the items he had used to describe himself. Like S-1, he added several others which appear to take account of the social task facing a youth minister: to get others' attention, to reflect, to be unbothered by self doubt. Such ministers, I-1 believed, are outgoing and not easily flapped.

I-1 reported an even more severe winter constriction than did S-1. The only attribute he used to set ministers apart was the need to be unbothered by self doubt. Obviously that commodity was not scarce in their experience at that time.

Springtime brought a rebound to I-1, though a seasoned one. His final profile pared down the special attributes of a minister to youth to two: the need to relate to others and the need to reflect. Overall, such ministers need to be outgoing and not easily flapped. I-1 had begun with a laundry list and, after passing through a storm, had settled on a low profile, manageable role perception.

In the fall, I-1 perceived the youth he served in much more normal terms than did S-1. These youth need to act independently, to be assertive, to get others' attention, to relate to others, to get their due, to cope with stress and to get quick gratification. This profile at no point approaches two standard deviations from the norm. It is not far off from what most folk might attribute to the "excesses" of youth. I-1 saw the needs to cope with stress and to relate to others as the core: these he reported on each profile.

But I-1 did not maintain a remarkably stable profile as did S-1. The winter profile saw a shift from getting one's due to submitting to others' wishes. It further personalized the youth by adding the need to solicit emotional support from others and the need to be wary of close ties with others. The general descriptors reveal a deterioration of the fall's "normal" perception of youth. Now I-1 saw the youth to be self depricating and pessimistic about the future.

Springtime brought an even more radical flip-flop in I-1's perception of youth. Only the need to relate to others remained from earlier profiles. But the need to cope with stress was replaced by the need to reflect. And both general descriptors became inverted. Now youth were characterized as outgoing and not easily flapped. All three shifts approached or exceeded statistical significance.

Perhaps it is not surprising that an intern should exhibit more severe shifts than a supervisor in perception about self, minister and youth. I-1's self and minister profiles shift in ways somewhat similar to the shifts of S-1, reflecting both the crises of parish life during the year and, perhaps, the deep sharing of clinical supervision. Whereas S-1 maintained a core of stability in each set of profiles, I-1 "migrated" in his perception of self from fall to spring, substituting the need to be in charge for the need to help others. In addition, I-1 seemed, during the year, to focus and settle into a manageable perception of minister to youth.

The major difference between supervisor and intern came in the profiles of youth they served - and the difference was major. S-1 presented an almost rigidly even perception of the youth over time. Virtually nothing changed. I-2 reflected frustration with the youth in the winter profile and a remarkable turn-around in the spring. In fact, the spring youth profile is identical with the spring minister profile. It is clear from the interviews that I-1 had come to the view that ministry involved the empowering of others to minister. It is also clear that he had experienced ministry from his youth. However, it may be well to be a bit wary of the sentiment which accompanied the spring shift. Ought the particular experiences of response and fellowship that I-1 experienced from his youth, and the role affirmation he gained from individual parents and school officials be translated into such a benign perception of youth in these difficult circumstances? Might clinical supervision's powerful focus on personal empowerment require a supplement which draws more direct attention to systemic and contextual features of physical and social existence?

THE SECOND DYAD

At the beginning of the project, Supervisor Two (S-2) perceived himself with as much instrumentality as S-1 had nurturance. The strongest perception (which remained core throughout the year) was the need to act independently. The fall profile was completed with the need to be assertive, to get others' attention, to take risks, to get one's due, to be wary of close ties with others.

The winter profile remains substantially the same with the addition of a couple of task items: the need to be in charge and to do well. The wariness of others is replaced (and explained) by the need to agonize over the meaning of relations with others. By springtime, the profile has been refined to support the need to act independently with the need to avoid routine and to take risks.

S-2 sees himself as an independent and active agent whose task it is to make a difference in a difficult and fluid setting.

In the fall, S-2 perceived the minister to youth to need to reflect and to be in charge. In general he saw these ministers as outgoing and not easily flapped. This was a core profile which served S-2 throughout the year. There was no overlap in the factors S-2 attached to his fall profiles of himself and minister to youth. In fact, in his interview, he asserted "I am not a minister." One ought not to expect the close relation between self and role observed in S-1.

By wintertime, S-2 had added several items to his fall core, reflecting the circumstances of keeping in touch with his youth. In addition to being reflective and in charge, ministers to his youth need to avoid routine, help others, relate to others, get others' attention and get quick gratification. There is virtually no overlap with S-2's expanded winter perception of himself.

The springtime profile continues the same, consistent core pattern, though the interpersonal items are eliminated. The needs to get quick gratification, to relate to others, and to get others' attention are replaced by the needs to do one's job, to get one's due and to be unbothered by self doubt. Even the minister, concluded S-2, needs to be primarily instrumental.

S-2 followed S-1 in perceiving the youth themselves to be noticeably different on many variables. However his fall profile was not so extreme. He listed 9 scale scores, only one of which was statistically significant. Youth, perceived S-2, need to be high profile but leary of relationship. They are in constant flux. He sees them as self deprecating and pessimistic about the future.

S-2 maintained virtually the same profile at the winter scoring, though, interestingly, with a more deviant scoring on almost all items. To this core he added several relational items: the need to be diffident, to solicit emotional support from others, to submit to others' wishes and to keep people at a distance. .

The spring profile eliminated some of the items S-2 perceived to make youth high profile and leary of relationships, but the pattern remained.

S-2 himself had a history of experience with street youth, both in his own youth and in his professional development. It is probable that, as a young professional, he identifies closely and realistically with them. His view of himself and of ministry (which is not how he perceives his work role) is driven, we believe, by his experience and perception of street youth. He is clear about the burden of the social circumstances in which they live and believes that a realistic appraisal of those circumstances is needed if street youth are to be served. S-2 has opted for instrumentality over relationship in his supervision. He has been unwilling to cloud the former with the latter, as the interviews make clear.

At the beginning of the project, Intern Two (I-2) perceived herself to need to reflect and to relate to others. She saw herself as outgoing and not easily flapped. It is interesting to notice that this is the same profile I-1 developed for minister to youth at the end of the year.

I-2 maintained the reflective and relational core in her winter self profile. However, she stopped perceiving herself as especially outgoing, and began to see herself as needing to avoid risks and conflicts. She continued to see herself as not easily flapped.

By springtime, the only special self-attribution I-2 made was that she is not easily flapped.

The interview data revealed a field and supervision experience that I-2 found surprising and difficult to handle. We interpret her winter self-perception to be defensive, and her spring profile to indicate a withdrawal of herself into a place where she did not need to extend herself in any special way. Her perception of herself, given the chaos of street ministry and of an instrumental style of supervision, resulted in a single special profile item, the descriptor of being not easily flapped.

I-2 began her internship with a sparse perception of the role of minister to street youth. She emphasized only the general descriptor, outgoing. By wintertime, she added needs to be reflective, to relate to others, to help others and to avoid routine. But by the time of the spring profile, the only need remaining was the need to relate to others. Even the general descriptor as outgoing had been absorbed. By springtime, the role of minister to youth carried about the same general description for I-2 as it had at the beginning of her internship.

I-2 began her internship year with a profile of youth which was virtually identical with that of her supervisor. She also saw street youth as needing to be high profile and leary of relationships.

By winter time the need to be assertive had been replaced by a lack of confidence. In addition, the need to be unbothered by self doubt was transformed into the need to solicit emotional support from others. I-2 no longer perceived youth to need to agonize over the meaning of relations with others, and a new item, the need to avoid routine, surfaced as a strong descriptor. In this variety of ways, I-2 perceived that the youth needed her more. The major problem she saw with getting her style of ministry off the ground with street kids, repeated contact over time, also surfaced in the kids' need to avoid routine. Nonetheless, I-2 appeared to be ready to struggle with ways to do her kind of ministry with these kids.

I-2's spring profile shows a considerably different perception of youth. No longer are they especially pessimistic about the future. The need to be wary of close ties with others has been replaced by the need to relate. The needs to be assertive and to get one's due have been added. The need to solicit emotional support from others and the need to lack confidence have both been dropped. The texture of the spring profile is of more competent youth. This may have been a useful perception for an intern who had moved her ministry from the youth to the staff.

The second dyad struggled with each other throughout the year. There was simply no overlap in their profiles of themselves at the beginning of the year, and this did not change. Throughout the year, S-2 perceived ministers with youth to need to be in charge and to be reflective. This profile was enlarged during the year to include several relational items. By winter, I-2 developed a profile for minister to youth which substantially matched that of S-2; however, by springtime, her profile had shrunk to include only one noticeable item. It is important to remember that S-2 refused to classify himself as a minister. It seems that it took I-2 half the year to become convinced of this. She tried hard to relate to S-2 using the ministerial role she brought with her. This was offensive to S-2 and he kept challenging that role. She found very little left in his style of work to emulate. It is clear that S-2 was not effective in making sharp for I-2 the instrumental character of his contribution as supervisor. He could not, he felt, give her what she wanted. She wanted a clinical style of supervision. She was prepared to accept nothing else. Both left the year professionally distant from one another, having agreed to simply meet as friends.

The second dyad began with virtually identical views of the youth they served. S-2 maintained a core view of youth throughout the year while I-2 modified her view as she sought, unsuccessfully, to apply the view of ministry she brought with her. Her perception of the youth, rather than her view of ministry, changed. Unfortunately, the change was in a direction that permitted I-2 to withdraw from active relations with the youth. She was not able to learn, instrumentally, how to interpret the predicament of and how to work with street youth. These understandings and skills which her supervisor offered were not available to her.

* * * * *

The Adjective Check List data revealed interesting patterns of how dyad members saw themselves, the role of minister to youth and the youth they served.

Dyad S-1/I-1 revealed important shifts in their personal relationship during the year. S-1 saw himself and minister to youth role as congruent, in each case emphasizing relational attributes. During the dark days of winter, there was a certain retrenchment in his perception of his social attributes, but most of these perceptions returned by spring. S-1 kept a tenaciously negative view of the youth which did not change throughout the year.

I-1 began the year reporting his need to be social and in charge, and he marked a long laundry list of attributes necessary for ministers with youth. During the year (and the pain of winter) I-1's perception of himself was truncated, but rebounded by spring. His profile of ministers with youth constricted severely in winter and rebounded into a carefully focused twosome by spring: to relate and to reflect. But most strikingly, I-1 shifted markedly from fall to winter in his perception of youth; and radically, from winter to spring. He began the year viewing the youth as relatively normal; became heavily discouraged with them by winter; but came to see them with strong positive traits by spring.

One difference between the supervisor and the intern was in the profiles of youth they served - and the difference was major. S-1 presented an unchanged perception of the youth over time. I-1 reflected frustration with the youth in the winter profile and a remarkable turn-around in the spring. In fact, I-1's spring youth profile is identical with his spring minister profile. I-1 had come to the view that ministry involved empowering others to minister. By then he had experienced personal responsiveness from his youth.

However, one must be a bit wary of the sentiment which accompanied I-1's spring shift. Should I-1's experiences of response and fellowship with his youth, along with the role affirmation he gained from individual parents and school officials be translated into such a benign perception of marginalized youth? Does supervision focused on personal empowerment also require a supplement which draws more direct attention to systemic and contextual features of life in the ghetto?

The second dyad (S-2/I-2) was far less relational than the first dyad. S-2 saw himself to be instrumental - characterized by the need to act independently. This perception remained all year. His view of minister (a role he did not identify for himself) reflected instrumentality - the minister needs to reflect and to be in charge. Like S-1, he viewed youth in realistic, negative terms, and his perception changed little over the year.

I-2 began the year perceiving herself to be reflective and related to others. These traits overlap with S-2's view of a minister's role. By springtime these traits were not central for her. She found, instead, that she was not easily flapped. We understand this pattern to be a defensive withdrawal. She moved from the chaos of street ministry and from an instrumental style of supervision to a personally circumscribed, less disorienting frame of interpretation. During the year, I-2 had a sparse view of ministers with youth. They were basically outgoing. This view remained constant. I-2's perception of youth matched her supervisor's in the fall. By winter, I-2 viewed youth as needing her more, in a variety of ways. This is the same idea of ministry she applied to her supervisor during this time. By spring she came to view the youth as considerably more competent - a shift we interpreted as a defensive one, in the light of her reduced contact with youth.

The second dyad struggled together throughout the year. There was no overlap in their profiles of themselves at the beginning of the year, and this did not change. Throughout the year, S-2 perceived ministers with youth to need to be in charge and to be reflective. This profile was enlarged during the year to include more aspects of relationship. By winter, I-2 developed a profile for minister to youth which substantially matched that of S-2; however, by springtime, her profile had shrunk to include only one personal item. It is important to remember that S-2 refused to classify himself as a minister. I-2 tried hard to minister to S-2 using the ministerial role she brought with her. This was offensive to S-2, and he kept challenging that role. She found very little in his style of work to emulate. S-2 was not effective in making clear for I-2 how the instrumental character of his supervision style contributed to her work as a minister. He could not, he felt, give her what she wanted. She wanted a clinical style of supervision. She was prepared to accept nothing else. Each finished the year professionally distant from the other, agreeing to simply meet as friends.

The second dyad began with virtually identical views of the youth they served. S-2 maintained a core view of youth throughout the year while I-2 modified her view as she sought, unsuccessfully, to apply the view of ministry she brought with her. Her perception of the youth, rather than her view of ministry, changed. Unfortunately, the change permitted I-2 to withdraw from active relations with the youth. She was not able to learn how to interpret the predicament of and how to work with street youth instrumentally. These understandings and skills which her supervisor offered were not integrated into her experience of ministry.

Thinking About Ministry:
patterns revealed by "organizing metaphors" used by the supervision dyad

In their book, Metaphors We Live By, (Chicago: University of Chicago Press, 1980) George Lakoff and Mark Johnson present a theory of metaphor which extends beyond modern literary and philosophical debates on the subject. They describe how metaphors structure the ways humans think, "...we have found....that metaphor is pervasive in everyday life, not just in language but in thought and action. Our ordinary conceptual system, in terms of which we both think and act, is fundamentally metaphorical in nature" (p.1).

These scholars draw on the common language available to everyone and notice how certain foundational (or perhaps "root") metaphors constrain communication. By listening to the ways in which people talk with each other, they have been able to identify several common English metaphors. The following examples illustrate their approach:

ARGUMENTS ARE WAR   He attacked every point I made.
                     I shot holes in his plan.
                     We squared off across the table.
                     He conceded the point.
                     I blew him out of the water.

WORDS ARE CONDUITS   The meaning is in the words.
                     Your words are empty of thought.
                     The words must convey your sentiments.

KNOWLEDGE IS A POSSESSION   I have all the facts right here.
                           I've got what it takes to land that job.
                           No one can take my experience away from me.

LIFE IS A CONTAINER   She had a full life.
                      Life is empty without you.
                      Her life is jammed with activities.
                      Nothing in life is worth that.

TIME IS MONEY   He spent all his time shooting pool.
                She wasted her time on him.
                Our time together was profitable.

    Lakoff and Johnson, like more traditional metaphor scholars, maintain that a metaphoric process takes the common knowledge of one well-known sphere of experience (the source domain) and maps or transfers this knowledge onto experience which is less familiar or undefined (the target domain). Concepts of time, life, knowledge and persuasive arguments remain mysterious dimensions of human life, yet they are rendered more comprehensible when likened to money, containers, war and possessions. Lakoff and Johnson claim that these metaphoric thought structures are acquired and practiced through every day language and communication contexts.

    In addition, Lakoff and Johnson claim that no single metaphor can be fully mapped from the source domain to target domains. There is always something left unexplained in the target domain experience. Thus, several metaphors must work together to provide adequate explanations of the target domain.

    Ministry is one of those mysterious (and sometimes chaotic) target domains which requires a number of source domains to describe its many dimensions. In this research, we assumed that one (or several) source domains are preferred by the participants and structure his/her experience and thinking about ministry. In reviewing the autobiographies, the logs and the interviews, dominant metaphors for each participant have been identified. Several minor, or less significant, metaphors have been noted as well. What is of interest here is the range and structure of the metaphors used by each participant, and the "match" of metaphors between supervisor and intern.

    We have looked at three types of written texts: reports of (1) what the participants do as ministers; (2) what the participants think or feel about ministry; (3) what the church is and does (which shapes the participant's ministry). From these written or transcribed texts we have recorded recurring words, phrases and ideas, and from these have identified the dominant metaphors of thought. Our method of analysis builds on the unpublished work of the following scholars: Dedre Gentner and Jonathan Grudin, "The Evolution of Mental Metaphors in Psychology: a Ninety-Year Retrospective," 1982; Naomi Quinn, "American Marriage and the Folk Social Psychology of Need Fulfillment," 1985; and Naomi Quinn, American Marriage: A Cultural Analysis, 1985.

    The following 19 frequently repeated metaphors have been identified from common phrases used by supervisors and interns in our study. They will be used in our analysis to help us understand how participants thought about ministry. (See Appendix 3 for examples of each metaphor.)

Minister as Parent

Minister as Teacher
Minister as Agent
Minister as Priest
Minister as Helper
Minister as Savior
Minister as Healer
Minister as Communicator
Minister as Translator
Minister as Counselor
Minister as Witness
Minister as Jesus Christ
Minister as Friend
Minister as Wounded or Weak People
Minister as Servant
Minister as Namer
Minister as Role
Minister as Entity
Minister as Persona

THE FIRST DYAD

The most important metaphors which structure Supervisor One's (S-1) notions of ministry are Minister as Agent, Entity, and Wounded/Weak Person. While S-1 showed signs of thinking of the minister as Counselor, Priest, Translator, Teacher and Helper, these metaphors were not dominant.

In S-1's thought the minister is an Agent, a person who sets things in motion. The minister responds to the needs he sees in people by encouraging better communication, and seeking to deepen the relationships or the learning of congregational members. The Agent minister perceives the "needs" of the congregational members by relating to them, and sets people into motion to alleviate those needs. He/She is not concerned with carrying out a personal agenda, but seeks to carry out the agenda of the congregation.

S-1's metaphor of Agent blends with another metaphor, perhaps one which is prior in his thought: minister as Entity. This abstract notion (one which S-1 never uses directly) places the person of the minister at the center of ministerial activity. What the minister feels, thinks, values, experiences, and the gifts and/or skills the minister has shape, the ways in which one defines the situation of ministry. The minister takes the fullest extent of his/her self into the situation of ministry. The self or Entity acting within the situation can then become the Agent.

The minister as Namer also underlies S-1's thought. The minister names the gifts found in others, names feelings, articulates the dynamics of a situation and various plans of action. As an Entity or self interacting in the context, the minister names the "needs" present and goes into action to activate resources for change.

S-1 also thinks of the minister as a Wounded/Weak Person. He reported instances throughout the year when he was in pain or failed to meet the needs presented by the congregation or the intern. He recognized these as important aspects of his ministry. This meshes with the metaphor of minister as Entity, for it places the "bad" experiences of ministry within the total experience of the ministering person. A minister may act from his/her own pain in ways which may be called ministry. This metaphor also extends the metaphor of Namer, for often the minister must name the pain and its sources before acting.

All of these metaphors correlate nicely with S-1's ACL characteristics. Relating to people and situations are necessary aspects of these metaphors. They were evident in S-1's reports throughout the year, but the minister as Entity and Namer metaphors became more prominent in his thinking later in the year.

S-1's thinking reflects a clinical model of training which is context and person oriented. Ministry takes place in face-to-face situations. An action can be called ministry to the extent that it utilizes the gifts and experiences of the minister who names her/his own needs and the needs of those ministered to accurately.

Intern One (I-1) used five metaphors dominantly throughout the year: the Minister as Agent, Parent, Communicator, Translator and Teacher. But the focus of his relationships and actions shifted somewhat as his thinking changed.

I-1 understands himself as someone who takes charge, gets people hooked up with social and church resources and organizes activities. Fulfilling the needs of others is dominant in his understanding of the ministry of the church, and thus shapes his thinking on pastoral ministry. Initially he was comfortable serving as an Agent for the youth and the families of the housing project where he worked. But when he finally realized that he was perceived by the church as a mister-fix-it man, the focus of agency enlarged. He became a relationship forming agent between church members and the youth. By the end of the year he felt as if he had succeeded in getting some church members involved with the youth from the housing project, something they would not have done on their own.

Particularly with regard to youth, I-1 took over many tasks appropriate for Parents, and expressed his feelings for the youth he saw at the tutoring center in parental ways. He set up school appointments for various youth and attended the appointments with the youngsters. (He made no mention of whether or not the youth's natural parent(s) attended.) He defended a youth's rights to make his/her own decision about a placement, going against the first decisions of the youth's natural parent. When "rejected" by several youths he had tutored, he discovered his great love and care for them. They were his kids.

The minister as Agent and Parent metaphors compliment each other and extended I-1's thinking on ministry. Both center on the "needs" of other people. Had I-1 related only to adults, the Parent metaphor would not have been so dominant. But the age differential between the intern and most of the youth he worked with naturally set a parent-child relationship structure. Knowing the developmental and social tasks of youth (regardless of their marginality) and recognizing the "needs" of the housing project youth made this metaphor more prominent in I-1's speech and writing.

I-1 reported that many of his interactions with people in the housing project centered around talking; he was a Communicator. Many of these communications were pragmatic, focusing on some problem or following up on some incident. He typically had "conversations," "spoke to the youth," "talked with a parent" in various contexts around the projects or at the church. However by the end of the year he used "sharing" rather than "talking" in his logs, to discuss his "communications" with the youth. He shared his plans, his feelings, his expectations with the youth in particular. He continued communicating with people about problems and situations, but he also began to communicate more regularly his own personal thoughts and feelings.

The Translator metaphor extends the communicator metaphor. I-1 understands his role as minister to include explaining to the youth why people do certain things: why the school expects them to attend, why they must study to achieve professional goals. He explained to the church people why youth needed certain types of experiences or bridged the worlds of the youth from the housing project and the adults of the church. The Translator mediates between worlds, which is how I-1 understands the traditional role of the Black pastor. While still communicating with people within both worlds, I-1 often stood on the boundary of each. He understood the "white" way of doing things and yet was "Black" in the white's eyes. In his communications he was a conduit through which one could come to an understanding of another.

The Teacher metaphor was prominent in I-1's thinking and extends both the Communicator and Translator metaphors. It also links with the Agent metaphor. I-1 understands one of his primary responsibilities in the housing project and in the church to be teaching people skills and/or knowledge which empowers them to better their situation. Teaching can lead to the alleviation of some needs and clear the way for better communication. He sought to "give" people the necessary "facts" so that they might become independent, self-determining agents. Though his actual experience in the housing project shows some tension in dealing with the youth's independence, he nevertheless did not want to stay in a dependent, Agent or Translator relationship with the youth.

These metaphors were dominant throughout the year in I-1's thinking and showed their roots in his earlier experiences with delinquent youth in the East. They are quite consistent with his ACL characterization of ministers, which focused primarily around the need to relate. I-1 is a face-to-face minister who moves from context to context, acting as an agent of change, but without always identifying the needs or problems of the youth

correctly.
    In the face of his failure to identify the needs of the youth or the parents of the housing project project accurately, I-1 added a new metaphor to his thinking on ministry: minister as Wounded/Weak Person. As the year progressed, in supervision and in his relationships around the project, he acknowledged his own inadequacy and fears. He came to realize that much of this activity as Agent was a way of defending against his own vulnerability. He reported becoming more comfortable sharing his feelings with the youth and touching some of his own pain. He gained enough strength from his supervisory experience and freedom in working with the youth so that he began pressing other students in NCSCM to explore their own places of pain and its relationship to ministry. His dominant metaphors are now colored by this metaphor of weakness: his Agency has limits; his Communications express feeling; and his Translations bring people together in relationships which endure after he leaves.

* * * * *

    S-1 and I-1 structure their thinking on ministry in very similar ways. Both began the year thinking of ministers as Agents, but in nuanced fashions. As the year progressed they both came to think of ministers as wounded, weak or limited persons who needed the resources and gifts of others to survive. S-1 had known this before but had to remember this earlier learning. I-1 learned and integrated this experience into his thinking during the year. They both worked from a clinical model of training. Ministry occurs in the specific situation; ministry employs the gifts of the minister; ministry meets specific needs and defines actions and thoughts. Their responsibilities did not change during the year; the roles which they were hired to fill remained constant. The focus of their ministries were different. S-1's focus was primarily on the congregation; I-1's focus was on the projects and its relationship to the church. Yet they shared common ways of thinking with regard to the nature of ministery and were able to come together, share with each other and teach each other thus extending the other's thinking on the role and nature of ministry with marginalized people.

THE SECOND DYAD

    Supervisor Two (S-2) showed the fewest metaphors for ministry of any team member. Two dominate his thinking: minister as Role and minister as Persona. He views the church as an institution, primarily, and thus, ministers carry out the roles the institution requires in a specific setting. He claims that he is not a minister because he is not working in a church. He does not have the traditional "symbols" needed to identify him as a minister. He is quite emphatic that the seminary intern is on the site to do a job, a job defined by the needs of the clients and staff related to "spiritual" issues. It is a role, an ad hoc role, within the organization. The Center is structured to serve primarily the physical and psychological needs of youth.
    S-2 recognizes that role tasks are carried out by living people who exhibit a Persona. He identified preaching, praying, etc., as appropriate ministry activities without identifying specific institutional contexts in which they are performed. It is "okay" for the seminary intern to pray at the end of their supervision session because she feels the need to express her Persona in that way in that setting. But he did not see this to be consistent with (or required in) his role as director. He admits to hiding behind his role as director, covering many aspects of his own Persona with the staff. The seminary intern could relate to the clients and staff around theological/spiritual issues in a way which was consistent with her own temperament and convictions. Her role as intern was shaped by her Persona.
    S-2's primary metaphor for supervision is Translator. He saw his task and strength with I-2 to be his ability to process or translate her theological language into "street" experience. He also understood one of his tasks as director to be meeting with churches and doing some "reverse mission." This thinking is in keeping with S-2's Role notion of ministry and the institutional demands of that role. He is not a minister because his Role at the Center is different.
    The minister as Agent figures somewhat into S-2's thinking about ministry, though it

is not as dominant as the other two. He hints that the metaphors of Witness, Friend, and Helper may be creeping into his thinking about what a minister is and does, but they are not firmly established. They are also borrowed from the intern.

S-2 separated himself from the church because of certain "theological" issues he can not resolve. He feels the Church does not offer adequate answers to his questions. He played a number of doctrinal sparring games with the intern, but he was not actually invested in them. His dominant metaphors remained constant throughout the year. The theological debates he and the intern engaged in during the year seemed to give him some new things to consider. By the end of the year, he acknowledged the intern's metaphors for ministry as being acceptable for her, but maintained his Role-Persona structure. This thinking is reflected in his ACL characteristics, particularly the need to be in charge (role); to do one's job (role); to relate to others (persona) and to be self-confident (persona). S-2's thinking is structural, theoretical and administrative. Ministry is a role defined by the combination of tasks the institution must accomplish for its survival.

Intern Two (I-2) began the year with a number of active metaphors in her thought and generally settled into three or four dominant ones. Initially minister as Agent, Teacher, Parent, Helper, Translator, Witness and Friend could be found in her writings. However by the end of the year minister as Witness, Jesus and Servant predominated, with hints of minister as Translator remaining. In her autobiographical report I-2 gave very little indication of how she thought about ministry prior to going to the Center, indicating only that her church needed to reach out to different people. At the Center she was going to "go-with-the-flow."

I-2's early attempts to talk about spirituality and morality at the Center met with rebuff and criticism. She reported confusing messages sent by staff and clients about their understanding of ministry. She began using the metaphor of Witness by mid-fall. She planned not to press "religious" issues; her love and care for the clients, and her own integrity, were her Witness.

While I-2 wrote and spoke of her faith in typically doctrinal (Baptist) terms, she never likened herself to Jesus. However, the incidents she reported and her attitudes toward prostitutes and gays can be easily paralleled with the stories of Jesus, reported in the Gospels. She patiently endured anti-church harangues, gave caring but honest Biblical interpretations on homosexuality, etc., and basically provided a presence of "grace" to the staff. This metaphor is foundational to her use of Friend, Helper and Parent metaphors.

The metaphors of Witness and Jesus are closely related and share common territory in I-2's notion of "presence." She is present to the staff and clients in times of crisis (as a friend) and is a "presence" at the Center as she witnesses to her faith by her actions and conversations. Her thinking is very consistent with her Baptist background and its "priesthood of believers" theology.

The metaphor of Servant crept in I-2's reports in the second half of the year. Servant in this context has a different connotation than in other writings on ministry. The passive "on-call" nature of servanthood is emphasized; servants are at the beck and call of masters. They have no other plans than to respond to the needs of others. I-2 reported many of her ministry experiences to be responses to the summons of her supervisor, the clients or staff. It is in the situation of acting as Servant that she often acts as Translator, explaining how her faith and understanding of God can make sense in painful situations. These two metaphors are consistent with the Witness-Jesus metaphors, for it is when she is called upon by others that she can Witness or act as Jesus to others. The metaphors of Witness and Jesus in I-2's thinking presuppose the Servant metaphor. All of these metaphors require an ability and disposition to relate to others.

I-2's primary metaphors are passive in mood. She responded to others' needs; she did not initiate programs. She did not think in terms of "priestly" things. Her actions are diffuse and structured by her own temperament and reading of the other person(s) involved. The institution of the church or religion does not influence her thoughts on ministry significantly. Ministry is personal and intimate. It is _personally_ demanding. Ministers touch (and possibly heal) the psychic pain of others.

* * * * *

The metaphors operating in S-2's and I-2's thinking can not easily be joined; they do not make a common "pool" of metaphors which can structure their joint understandings of what ministry is or what ministers do. However, their individual metaphor "pools" compliment each other. One pool is framed by institutional needs; the other is anti-institutional. One pool focuses on task; the other focuses on persons. One pool relies on role; the other on the individual. Both pools are required when talking about ministry. However these pools of metaphorical thought did not overlap for S-2 and I-2. Each learned something about what and how the other conceived ministry. But neither one expanded his/her own thinking structure (and thus did not expanded his/her action patterns) with regard to ministry.

* * * * *

Even though several of these metaphors are shared in one way or another by the various team members, the contexts for ministry were quite different. This points out that the setting for ministry not only shapes thinking, it is the arena in which choices are made through which thinking is made manifest. Thinking and setting continually interact. The analysis shows how the metaphorical thinking of the supervisor and intern can converge in ministering to the marginalized and enhance the work of the other. It also shows how the differences of metaphorical thought between supervisor and intern in the same setting are not integrated. Both ministry settings presented a variety of action courses which the supervisors and interns could choose. Their reports showed that the way in which they thought of ministry narrowed their choices providing them some parameters within which to describe their actions and understandings. The ways in which they thought about ministry shaped their choices; the choices they made and the actions they took continued to expand their thinking.

<u>Training in Reflection</u>
Performative Language and Speech Acts
in Logs and Feedback to the Supervision Dyad

In the late 1950's, language philosopher John Austin noted that language could not be described solely in terms of its truth or falsehood (as the logical positivists contended). Austin expanded language analysis to include how language "did things." (<u>How To Do Things With Words</u>. Cambridge: Harvard University Press, 1962) He identified several ways in which utterances worked to accomplish various tasks which changed states of human affairs, such as pronouncing a man and woman married; swearing someone into office; christening a ship or a child. John Searle picked up on Austin's work in the late 1960s, particularly the social contextual aspects of performative language actions. <u>Speech Acts: An Essay in the Philosophy of Language</u> (Cambridge: Cambridge University Press, 1969, 1983) is his exploration into the "rules" of various social contexts which makes performative language speech actions possible.

As a philosophical endeavor, speech act theory has many problems that have not been satisfactorily resolved. Attention to specific contexts of language usage has shown that simple utterances may be interpreted on different levels. Thus, the obvious meaning of the utterance "it is raining" (description) may be intended to direct a young child to wear her raincoat to school when spoken by a mother in the morning as the child is ready to walk out the door. The conditions (or rules) of the situation, the intention of the speakers, and the desired effect of the utterance to be interpreted are all aspects of the speech act which must be considered.

However, Austin's basic insight that language "does things" or "performs things" has stimulated sociolinguists (cf. Richard Bauman, <u>Verbal Art As Performance</u>. Rowley, Ma.: Newbury House, 1977; Dell Hymes, <u>Foundations in Sociolinguistics</u>. Philadelphia: University of Pennsylvania Press, 1974) and anthropologists (cf. Ruth Finnegan, "How to Do Things With Words," <u>Man</u> 4:1969, 537-522; Stanley Tambiah, "A Performative Approach to Ritual," in <u>Culture, Thought and Social Action</u>. Cambridge, MA: Harvard University Press, 1985) to investigate the performative aspects of social interactions. Since the middle 1970s Speech Act theory and performative language studies have found their home in the broad field of linguistic pragmatics. (Cf. Stephen Levinson, Pragmatics. Cambridge: Cambridge University Press, 1983; Teun A. van Dijk, Text and Context. London: Longman, 1978).

Our work is a departure from most studies in performative language because of the written nature of the utterances made by the loggers and feedback writer. (Note: throughout this discussion "utterance" will be used to denote any written statements made by loggers or feedback writer. We recognize that "utterance" conventionally means something that is spoken; nonetheless, the term is preferable to "statement" which may be confused to mean a specific speech or performative action.) Writing extends the boundaries of the interaction context greatly, taking the interaction out of the immediate face-to-face or person-to-group setting. Writing presents a tight, cohesive unit of thought which can be more easily refined and analyzed by the writer and reader. The meaning of any written statement is not mutually constructed by the interactants, as is possible in verbal interaction (cf. John Gumperz, Discourse Strategies, Cambridge: Cambridge University Press, 1983). Writing, therefore, displays many features which parallel ritual language (cf. Niyi Akinnaso, "On the Similarities Between Spoken and Written Language," Language and Speech. 28: 4, 1985): language is bounded and performed in a structured social context and with clear role distinctions and actions to be accomplished. The written logging-feedback structure created a distinctive context of and for social relationships which called for various types of speech acts and performative utterances.

FEATURES OF THE LOGGING-FEEDBACK SOCIAL CONTEXT

1. Structure of the Logging-Feedback Process.

The logging procedure was conceived as a total activity unit which consisted of distinct "moments":

$$\text{ACTION--REFLECTION--NEW ACTION}_1\text{-REFLECTION--NEW ACTION}_2$$

The logs were meant to build recursively, giving the writer practice in reflection on ministry. The activity was designed to make the log writer (LW) conscious of his/her activity as a minister in a world of ministry.

When the feedback writer (FW) received the logs, he read each one and wrote a letter to the LW which included various comments, additional reflections, questions, etcs. This written feedback we called an "interruption" - a break-in to the loop of the LWs' reflective world. The total structure of the process was then conceived as:

$$\text{ACTION--REFLECTION--NEW ACTION}_1\text{-REFLECTION--NEW ACTION}_2 \ldots$$
$$\text{FEEDBACK} \qquad \text{FEEDBACK} \qquad \ldots$$

The logging procedure was to help team members report their ministry experiences in the Network and their growing self-awareness. The log was a systematic plan for reflection and encouraged a certain thinking process. Two different loops were set up in the process: the LW's action-reflection loop and the interactive loop created by the LWs' and FW's exchange of written material.

2. Roles Within the Logging-Feedback Process.

Within the structure diagrammed above, at least two roles were necessary. The first is that of the log writer who was to write weekly reflections on ministry experiences. The writer was to follow the log format as it was designed, and was instructed via group meetings of team members and in log feedback on using the format. This role was taken on by the interns and supervisors at the beginning of research and required a commitment to learn the logging skill through practice.

The role of the LW may be broken down further into interns and supervisors. While the log protocols were the same for each group, the type of logs rendered represented the unique ministry position of the LW. This group distinction is also reflected in the type of responses given in the feedback letters.

The second role position in the structure is that of feedback writer. His task was to provide commentary on the reflective process of the LWs. The purpose of the feedback was to "interrupt" or stimulate the LWs' thoughts and encourage further reflection; thus the FW acted as outside observer to the actions of ministry reported.

The legitimacy of each role position within the structure was recognized and valued by all participants. The distinctive nature of each role was insured by the logging structure itself and by the type of written materials produced by the participants in these two distinct roles.

3. Performative Language and Speech Acts in the Logs and Feedback

The process of cataloguing individual performative utterances is full of pitfalls. Several philosophers and linguists have attempted to develop taxonomies of utterances (cf. Austin's How To Do Things With Words, last chapter; Searle's Speech Acts; Michael Hancher, "The Classification of Cooperative Illocutionary Acts." Language in Society 8 (1979):1-14; R.G.D'Andrade, "Speech Act Theory in Quantitative Research on Interpersonal Behavior," Discourse Processes 8 (1985): 229-259). Yet no single system of categorization has been able to account for every type of speech act. However, within the structure of the logging-feedback process, certain types of speech acts are called for and evidenced. The very structure of the log itself pressed the LWs into performative action as they tried to account for their places in the world of ministry.

The format of the logs during the fall of 1986 consisted of the following elements requiring specific performative language or speech acts.

FOCUS STATEMENT: To identify or NAME a ministry role action
CONCERN STATEMENT: To ANNOUNCE, NAME or ASSERT the reason for attending to the specific role action
ILLUSTRATION: To DESCRIBE or NARRATE an experience of ministry related to the focus and concern statements
LEARNINGS: To ASSERT specific learning about self, clients, and role drawn from the illustration
DECISION: To PROMISE or COMMIT to an action when returning to the arena of ministry

The format gave the LW the opportunity to perform various acts of reflection which brought past experience into present conscious thought. The action began with a role-framed action and continued with a specific professional concern. The illustration translated the role frame objectively and provided the means for articulating learning and future action. The speech acts which express this movement were primarily naming, describing, asserting, and promising.

At midyear the log formats were adjusted to account for the LWs' actual behavior in log writing. Throughout the fall the LWs habitually began writing at the point of the illustration and worked "backward" through the concern and focus statements. The format was changed to enhance the potential for recursion without negating the process of encouraging role awareness. The steps and accompanying speech acts were:

GOAL: NAMING the role learning goal to which the LW was attending
ACTIVITY: DESCRIBING/NARRATING an activity which illustrated the goal
LEARNING: ASSERTING important insights or conclusions drawn from the activity
EVALUATION: ASSERTING the pertinence of the activity and the learning for the initial goal.

LWs were required to set goals that they would attend to for a month at a time. In this way a series of logs were written on a single concept; this permitted further concept development over a period of time. By setting role learning goals, the log writer achieved the frame from which to think about a variety of events. This was easier and more useful than attempting to generate specific role actions. The LW could see several events which illustrated role learning, thereby developing skill in linking the general concept with a specific goal.

The simplified learning shifted the focus from the various roles taken by the person while engaging in ministry, some of which did not jibe easily with the goal the activity illustrated. The task was to assert a learning from the activity framed by the role learning which the log was reflecting.

The evaluation, like the decision, pressed the log writer to think about future action. However, an assertion has a different force than promising or commiting. The change was meant to perpetuate the action-reflection-action loop, making it more evident in the LW's daily work, and highlighting the recursive elements of the logging experience.

While the formats required similar speech activity and intention, the content of the actions were different. What should be noted here is that content or thought found in various speech acts might vary without changing the force or nature of the speech act. Many things may be named, but the force of the naming action remain; many things may be asserted, but the force of the asserting action is constant. Something has been done, something has changed.

The feedback letters did not follow a carefully prescribed format. Generally in the fall the FW commented on the items of the log format point by point, either instructing the LW in using the format more effectively or picking up on the LW's utterances. During the spring the FW did not instruct LWs in writing the logs often, but rather picked up on various ideas, concepts, themes, or actions of interest. Because the feedback was instructive or impressionistic (See Stimulus Value section below) the speech acts of the FW were far more difficult to categorize.

During the fall, log and log feedback discourse was examined and categories were induced which we believed would help us understand the relationship between LW and FW. The result of this examination was a "Guideline for Content Analysis" (Appendix 4). Portions of that Guideline were applied to the Spring material studied here. Specifically, categories revealing speech acts were used. Altogether, there are three Appendixes which inform this analysis: Appendix 4 presents the guidelines used in log and log feedback content analysis. Appendix 5 presents four verbatim examples of the text of logs and log feedback. Appendix 6 presents the material in Appendix 5 coded for speech acts. Admittedly, at this stage, the categorizing is very intuitive and requires much more precision for future testing, but this attempt proved helpful in identifying the type and range of utterances made in the feedback letters.

The procedure used in determining the speech act list (Appendix 6) began by taking each sentence of the material individually and noting what the sentence was doing in the context of the paragraph and in the interaction between LW and FW overall. The range of performative utterances was quite narrow. Asserting, describing, elaborating, questioning, and, interpreting were the most frequent activities noted. After identifying an individual utterance type according to the guideline definition, the sentence was reevaluated in the paragraph context in which it was found. It times it was necessary to change the original decision on this second look particularly with elaboration statements. In isolation an utterance may appear as an assertion or perhaps a description, but in the wider context of the paragraph it may clearly elaborate an idea presented in the preceding sentence. (This larger context notion, or cohesion, is borrowed from Michael Halliday and Ruqaiya Hasan's book, Cohesion in English. London: Longman, 1976.) Elaborating does not appear on any of the taxonomies mentioned earlier; however, in the feedback context, there is referential and deitic evidence for such a speech action. The sentence-by-sentence analysis and sortings were compiled and basic impressions of the feedback action were formed.

The primary speech event of the feedback was letter writing. The writer was not bound by a particular format, but was constrained by the various speech acts given in the logs. (The name feedback itself notices a bounded arena of interactional possibilities.) While at first glance it appeared that the FW would have had a wide range of speech acts available to him to use, the range of actions was quite narrow. For Example, there were no specific examples of requesting or promising; few examples of interpreting or presenting facts.

4. Things To Note About the Logging-Feedback Context and Interaction

Because the feedback interruption took place in writing through the mail, the mutual construction of meaning possible in face-to-face interactions is limited. While the FW often asked questions in the feedback letters or gave directives, he had no way of knowing from the logs themselves whether these questions were answered by the LW or whether the directives were followed through. In addition, any confusion the LWs had as a result of reading the feedback letters could not be easily cleared up. However the letter form of feedback provided the opportunity for the FW to truly "interrupt" the Action-Reflection-Action loop due to the postponed delay. Receiving the feedback just prior to the due date of the next log set or just following it, forced the LW to recall the earlier logs written and re-reflect upon what s/he had written and done.

The difference in roles of the LWs and FW lead to different purposes in the written material produced by each. The log was meant as a report of a reflective process by the LW; feedback was given as a kind of commentary or dialogue, first with the writer's internal thought process in reading the log and then between the FW and LW. This difference led to an asymmetry of written material. Although there was no limit set on the length of a log, LWs usually confined their work to three-quarters of a page or less. The feedback, however, frequently went much longer. Usually the FW took more space to flesh out specific ideas than did the LW. The difference may be seen, in part, in the kinds of speech acts performed by the writers in both roles.

The level of personal address shifts within the logging-feedback process. The LWs used more formulaic language (particularly in the Focus, Concern, and Learning items or the Goal and Learning statements as directed by FW early in the fall.) Instruction in this formulaic language was meant to concentrate the LW's attention on his/her place in the world "in role." The log format did not explicitly call for such formal language, but it did strengthen the force of the speech act being performed in a given item on the format. The log was being performed for the sake of the writer, not for the sake of the reader. However, the FW's responses were addressed to the LW personally; the language of the feedback is not at all formulaic and is written clearly for the sake of the LW. The FW engages in many speech acts which are quite personal (calling the LW by name; thanking him/her, offering wishes of good luck, etc.).

Also of note and for further exploration is the limited range of speech acts performed by the FW in the feedback letters. The action of feedback began with the log report, and thus the experience of the LW first of all, and not with the world at large. The feedback, essentially in the form of commentary, does not engage in many speech acts which might traditionally be associated with teaching (i.e., instructing, directing, announcing, judging, arguing, or declaring "fact"). There is the real possibility that feedback which begins with the LW's (or student's, counselee's) reports or reflections do not exhibit a wide range of speech acts.

STIMULUS VALUE AND FEEDBACK RESPONSE

The preceding comments apply for the logging-feedback process and context in general. What follows here is a closer look at specific examples of logs and feedback from the Spring semester which demonstrate some interesting aspects of the LW-FW interaction. This body of material was selected because it (particularly the feedback) is not concerned any longer with training loggers into the use of the format. The FW, by his own admission, was freer to respond to the various ideas and concepts present in the logs and was not burdened with showing loggers how to improve their technical skills.

A total of 20 logs and feedback responses were sampled (I-1=6, I-2=4, S-1=6, S-2=4). This set represents all the logs dealing with the topic of supervision turned in by the LWs during the second semester.

Stimulus Value was the name we gave to the specific idea or issue that the feedback writer decided to elaborate on from the logs themselves. Since the logs were not addressed to the FW specifically and did not solicit any particular answers to problems, the FW was free to respond to a variety of issues. At times he picked on the same issue in consecutive letters, at times he chose a new idea for each paragraph. Certainly, there is an impressionistic quality about these responses, yet, the FW did not act capriciously. The purpose of feedback was always to stimulate additional thinking in the LW, thus the FW might press for clarity of thought or open up a new dimension of the LW's report for consideration.

While the catalogue of speech acts/ performative utterances was intially drawn up from the feedback letters, it also proved useful in identifying the types of sentences found the in the logs themselves. It was necessary to add the speech act "naming" to the catalog when dealing with the log material. (In the appendix see examples of four logs and feedback letters to note the range of things the FW wrote.) Looking at the speech acts within the logs and in the feedback letters as a whole the following generalizations can be made.

The supervision logs produced by I-1 and S-1 both engaged in descriptive speech acts in the activity section of their logs. They reported different sides of the supervision time they spent together, but the general sequence of sharing and insight gathering within their meetings were described. Their reports were given in the past tense and met the intention of the log format in this way. Both members of the dyad mastered the logging skill and performed the speech acts that each item called for.

I-2 and S-2, on the other hand, offered very little description of the supervision time together. They each used the logs to assert their own individual theological syntheses on various issues. Assertions were the most frequent speech acts in their logs. The present or active past tense characterized their log reports. I-2 tended to present only her perspective on things, not relaying S-2's viewpoint nor describing how the supervision interaction helped to clarify her position. S-2 tended more often to describe I-2's beliefs or assertions, but used them as a set-up in the log to assert his own viewpoints (his doubts as well as beliefs). Because S-2 presented both of their viewpoints, there is more evidence of the back-and-forth nature of their supervision session, though description is not the speech act which identifies his activity.

These two different types of performance tended to bring out different types of response from the FW. Overall, the speech event of feedback is characterized by speech acts elaborating themes found in the logs, asserting ideas which are related to but different from ones presented in the log, occasionally instructing the LW in how to write or think more clearly, or questioning the LW about what was written in the log or suggesting something different to consider.

Feedback to I-1 tended to extend themes and ideas which he described in the log. These extensions usually had something to do with ministry and the nature of learning how to be a minister. The FW also asserted some of his own theology occasionally as a way of illustrating his points.

Feedback to S-1 tended to extend themes he had described, but the extensions were colored by the FW's personal experience and personal theologizing. Often the feedback comments were centered on I-1's agenda in supervision, and less on S-1's "place" in the described setting. There were questions in the feedback to S-1, and most often they were questions related to the supervision process generally (i.e., What is processing? How do you help the student find his/her own solutions?)

Feedback to I-2 tended to be more instructional and questioning. She was pressed to describe more fully how she drew the conclusions she did in her logs. Her theological assertions seldom evoked personal sharing or theologizing from the FW. He cautioned her and gave gentle directives often, particulary in her management of pain and conflict.

Feedback to S-2 most often took the form of extending a theme or logically arguing toward an assertion (a pattern S-2 used often in his logs). Quesions which were raised took the form of challenge or moving on toward next steps in the supervision process. The FW shared his personal theological reflections with S-2 and used these as points of intersection, demonstrating a connection between S-2's "atheological beliefs" and his own "theological" ones.

Asserting, describing, questioning, directing, and restating are the most common speech acts found in the feedback speech event during the second semester (here listed in decreasing order of frequency). Asserting and describing are far and away the most numerous speech acts found. (See Appendix for count.) During the fall, interpretation and conjecture were more evident in the feedback letters than in the spring. Two reasons may account for this shift. First, in the fall, the FW's action was primarily instructing the LW in the logging process. He used interpretative statements and conjectural statements to "read between the lines" of the log reports to find its cohesive elements. Since he did not follow that pattern as closely second semester, the need for interpretative statements was reduced. Second, because the FW did not limit his remaks to the log formats themselves (as he had done first semester), he was more "up front," more "tranparent," in the second semester.

Speech acts and performative language analysis here has shown the character of utterances found in the logs and in the responses given in the feedback letters to each members of the two supervision dyads. When the logs and feedback letters were considered as individual units, the character of the engagement between the LW and FW can be seen, sometimes with surprising revelations.

SCHEMES OF RESPONSE

Earlier in section IV the different speech acts called for by the log format were noted. The format did not demand speech acts which were to engage the FW; the format was meant for the LW to engage him/herself in thoughtful reflection. The log was a schema for that reflection. However, no such scheme was prescribed for the FW. He responded to various ideas or concepts presented in the logs. Yet looking over the breakdown of feedback speech acts found, some partial patterns seem to be present.

Since the feedback letters were addressed to the LW and intentionally meant to stimulate his/her further reflection, features which encourage some level of interaction might be expected to be present. Certainly the acts of addressing the LW by name, thanking him/her and offering support leave no doubt that the FW is speaking to the LW. By describing to the LW what the log is about or what had taken placed in the log from the FW's viewpoint makes it clear that the focus of the feedback is primarily the arena of the LW's experience. However, the speech act most often employed by the FW to encourage further reflection is questioning. In many instances paragraphs in the feedback letters ended with one or more questions. These questions were of four types: clarifying, challenging, checking, or musing (where FW asks himself the question).

While questions often served to engage the LW's mind in further reflection, directives in the feedback letters served to stimulate some kind of action or encourage some kind of stance. The directives were most often in the form of suggestions, but the force of the speech act was to encourage additional activity on the LW's part.

Both of these engaging speech acts were nearly always preceded by some combination of speech acts, most often description -- elaboration -- assertion -- ... -- Question/Directive. The ellipsis above indicate that the description/assertion -- elaboration pattern could play back and fourth several times with a paragraph finally concluding with a question (or questions) or a directive.

While the log and feedback material of this study is too idiosyncratic to draw general conclusions, the patterns of speech acts in the feedback presents some possibilities for studying interaction teaching/coaching practices in other settings. Promising reflection/coaching sequence might look like these:

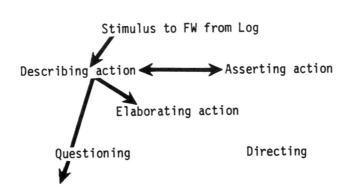

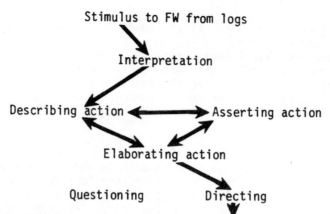

Stimulus to FW from logs

Interpretation

Describing action ←→ Asserting action

Elaborating action

Questioning   Directing

What is perhaps most significant about these emerging schemes is that the speech acts of asserting/describing, elaborating, interpreting, questioning and directing are the most frequent speech acts and are derived from the sequence of speech acts found in the LW's world of experience.

These emerging schemes should be tested and refined with other sorts of teaching/coaching examples to be found in classroom lectures, seminars, professor-student counseling appointments, therapeutic supervision sessions, etc.

LOOKING AT SPEECH ACTS AND PERFORMATIVE LANGUAGE IN THE LOGGING-FEEDBACK PROCESS

This analysis overall has uncovered much about the character of the logging-feedback process at the level of engagement and interaction. It has shown within this context the types of speech acts or performative langauge which encourage reflection and the types of linguistic action which can be elicited. Overall, the analysis of the structure of the logging-feedback process did not allow for clear evidence of changed behavior or thinking as a result of the feedback. (There is evidence in the interview tapes that indeed the feedback made a difference, but within the logs themselves this is not evidenced.) There is evidence at the technical level that the feedback served its instructive purpose in the fall by training the writers in certain formulas for performing certain speech acts.

The analysis opens the possibility of delving more deeply into the character of the interaction, particularly at the level of the FW. Noting the types of linguistic performances found in the feedback, certain emerging patterns are seen which warrant further testing. These patterns, it must be remembered, are found within a confined interactive logging-feedback structure and need certain refinements and changes if applied to other areas of teaching/coaching. Attention to the speech action, and less specifically to the content or proposition of an utterance, opens possibilities for generalizing potential schemas beyond certain disciplines.

The strength of this type of analysis lies not in its prescriptive or constructive nature, but in its power to illuminate "what's going on" within a context or social structure. It does not offer interventions as much as it sweeps aside assumptions about what is happening and demonstrates what is indeed happening. When this kind of "reality" has been revealed, the teacher, intern, supervisor, etc., stands on much firmer ground to make decisions as to how the learning/teaching interaction can be strengthened and enriched.

III. DISCUSSION

We have understood one critical component of professional schooling for ministry to involve the ongoing construction of social survival resources. Thus, learning will need to include basic skills in relating and in thinking, as they pertain to the tasks of ministry in the ministry setting.

We have understood our research to reflect a constructivist philosophical perspective, and therefore to admit forms of data gathering and analysis involving the intervention of the researchers. We are aware of a number of methodological difficulties that accompany "participatory" research. We have sought to cope with some of them in two ways.

Methodological Issues

AN ACTION SCIENCE PERSPECTIVE

First, we have chosen to define the contexts of our research using a series of feedback loops. The right to do such defining, we believe, comes with the constructivistic perspective of action science. The worlds we are studying are sociocultural worlds which exist and are generated through the interaction of persons.

Our struggle in seeking to operate this way is with the tradition within science of viewing the material studied as objects discrete from and over/against the investigator. This view usually extends to the atomization of what is studied. The units for study are judged to be simple, monadic units. Complex phenomena are assumed to be combinations of such units. They are generally not considered to be operational units themselves.

We have sought, in this study, to view complex units as operational. At one level, this permits us to see "word meanings" (in the mode of Vygotsky) as units for study; at another level, this permits us to see "worlds" (in the mode of Goodman) similarly.

It is our position that schooling which equips persons for professional practice takes place through the development of thoughtful relationships. When interactions are considered to be the units of investigation, relating and thinking can be studied in ways that inform teaching and learning for professional practice.

There are four loops we have used to conceptualize the sociocultural contexts of our study. First, we view each participant in the research in terms of the role(s) they bring with them to the alternative theological schooling experience. Faculty bring their role as classroom teacher. Supervisors bring their role as pastor/agency head. Interns bring their role as student. Part of the business of the alternative program is to challenge and interrupt these traditional roles. As this happens, participants may import other roles from their sociocultural past - e.g., parent, social activist, church member. Each of these constitutes an interactive "world" which contributes to the "world" of the alternative theological school.

For our project, we selected three interactions within NCSCM as arenas for data gathering. They were the interaction between intern and faculty in class; the interaction between intern and supervisor in supervision session; the interaction between intern and people served in work settings. By virtue of the structure of NCSCM, none of these arenas was the same as analogues provided in traditional theological schooling. Each required adaptation on the part of participants and came into functional existence as relationships stabilized over time.

A third loop was added through the design of our project. Participants were encouraged to give thought to their sociocultural contexts, and to generate data for the project, in part, through the development of a relationship with the project director. The director led monthly team meetings and wrote extensive responses to logs submitted as data.

A final loop was created between the project director and the research class which supported the project. Included in this loop is the relationship between the project director and his assistant which extended beyond the time of the class. Through this interaction the purposes and design of the research was explored, as it was carried out. This relationship permitted, for example, the inspection of the written feedback of the director to team members.

Logging exercizes were at the heart of the data gathering. These exercizes constituted an intervention into the alternative theological schooling. They also permitted the construction or elaboration of the four levels of relationship.

The logs, themselves, were instruments designed to bring to expression the way team members "thought in action." The concern was not simply to report on action; it was, rather, to reveal the log writer's frame for and evaluation of the action. It was, therefore, a format to invite learning through reflective action. To the extent that the log format was employed, and to the extent that evaluation impacted future activity, it became a device for the generation and maintenance of the interactions with which it dealt.

The content of each log was entirely open, but pulled for an experience in which the team member related in a role appropriate way (as intern, supervisor, faculty). The task seemed, on the surface, straightforward enough. However, every participant found it difficult to identify appropriate experiences and to contextualize them in professional learning ways.

A good bit of the difficulty lay, we believe, in the fact that NCSCM invited a consideration of relationships for which, despite years of experience in schooling, participants had no conventional language. They had what Vygotsky would call "operational knowledge" of their schooling and service interactions, but only "potential concepts" to describe them. The language of schooling provided many concepts related to theoretical and institutional life, but not so many related to the new sociocultural realities of NCSCM or the city. The logs uncovered this. They also gave participants a chance to generate concepts about ministry through which to make explicit their work both to themselves and others. As this occurred, new "worlds" were constructed for participants and for those with whom they worked.

Log feedback, written by the project director, began as an effort to support and train team members in log writing. The focus was on the logic of the log, and on language, introduced by the log writer, that might be adapted to make the logic clear. As concepts began to come into focus, the feedback came, also, to include "play" with those concepts - suggesting links with the worlds of religious tradition and team members' ministry settings.

It was the log feedback which made clear the importance of the last two loops mentioned above, for theological schooling. An interactional world, as any world, is taught and learned through public language. Operative relationships require conceptual form, if they are to be schooled. Efforts to give language to what one knows operatively can be supported by responsive conceptual "play." The process of this interaction requires, in turn, a monitoring relationship, to keep the schooling objective of language development for ministry clear and on track.

A VARIETY OF TECHNIQUES

The second way we have sought to cope with the methodological problems which accompany participatory research is to employ a variety of research techniques, with the thought that their juxtaposition will remind us of the limited value of each. This is easy to do at the design level, but more difficult to maintain as we interpret the results derived from one technique or another.

We have included four specific analyses. First, we have transcribed and examined the content of interviews to determine the experience of participants in supervision over time. We have displayed this self-report data without critical overlay. Second, we analyzed data from a standardized instrument given to team members three times over the year, to provide comparative information over time about their perception of persons in their schooling environment. Third, we have examined all the kinds of written documents we gathered to determine the metaphors for ministry which are latent in their language. Fourth, we have examined the structure and function of language in samples of the Logs and Log Feedbacks to determine how Log Feedback was stimulated and how role relations impacted that response.

None of the analyses is entirely satisfying in light of the sociocultural perspective of "action science." In each case the unit of investigation is too limited. The language of the interviews permits the introduction of "word meanings." These, however, were not assessed systematically. We assumed a shared meaning context, and therefore our ability to render participants' reports of the experience of supervision accurately. We are aware of the presence of bias both at the level of the reports and at the level of our rendering. For this project we have chosen to remain at the level of "common sense" in this analysis.

The Adjective Check List is a standardized instrument designed to compare the perceptions of a person with that of a normed population. As such it conceptualizes the person who completes it as an individual, with no attention to sociocultural context. It represents a quantitative strand of research in which meaning is inferred from statistical variation from the standard response of a "representative" pool. We have compared ACL data from each person with that provided by the dyadic partner. This helps us describe the dyadic relationship. However, all ACL data is derived from sources conceptualized to be individuals, and analyzed in ways appropriate to the comparison of an individual with a group.

The Metaphor Analysis seeks to be "qualitative." It lifts up precisely the issue of what an utterance "means" to the speaker. "Organizing metaphors" are posited which are not found in the utterance itself. Utterances are classified under these metaphors in order to suggest, descriptively and predictively, the pattern of meaning a person holds. This procedure rests on the use of intuitive judgement by the researcher, both at the level of naming the metsphors and at the level of classifying the utterances.

The Speech Act Analysis takes pains to clarify the social context for the language it classifies. Its categories are more public than the "organizing metaphors." But the effort to be precise about context and category narrows the generalizability of its results. The search for clarity of context inevitably falters, for we have found no way to exhaust the perception people have, even of the most precisely defined role relations. And the looser these definitions, the more uncertain the coding of language functions. In our study, language was coded intuitively, without inter-rater reliability checks. It was deemed preferable to rely on the comprehending judgment of an individual coder rather than to seek operational clarity about language function amongst a group of coders.

The limits confessed above are not intended to downplay the potential use of the results of our study. They are presented to make clear that communication research which takes the sociocultural context seriously cannot now, and may never be able to, achieve the precision expected when it is assumed that what is studied is a discrete object. As Argyris has pointed out, less precision does not preclude lack of rigor. This detailing of the limits of the level of precision or the level of generalizability in our analyses constitutes part of the rigor with which we have sought to study our subject. In the case of each analysis, we have sought to use procedures which reflect the assumptions of the method. We intend to have done each analysis well, within its rules of reference. It is the use we make of the results that we want to underline. This research, as an instance of "action science," places value on the setting of problems, as well as the solving of problems. We understand our effort to be exploratory - hence its descriptive center and the reliance on methods which involve intuitive judgements. We want to understand better how "practice" is taught and learned. The product of this study is a set of clarifying principles - an hermeneutic - around which schooling for practice can be organized. The results of each analysis will be considered to see what useful contribution they make to the formulation of the principles.

* * * * *

Our first three analyses produced a report of the nature and shape of supervision as experienced by partners in supervision. Without evaluating the benefits of supervision for each participant - a product which neither our intervention nor our analysis techniques permit - we are prepared to notice several features of the supervision interaction which we believe to be of interest for the design of professional schooling.

Most profoundly, we interpret our data to indicate that the supervision relationship developed over the year. Perhaps no relationship begins full blown; supervision certainly did not. The work of both parties in each dyad constituted a struggle with themselves and their work in the face of a partner. We have come to look on the supervision relationship as something generated over the year. It is built on the "worlds" that each party brought. The relationship itself is a construction - a "version of world" - built from the resulting interaction.

Our notion is that teaching and learning practice is a "world version producing" relationship. Its productivity arises in the process of such construction. We now turn to the principles which we believe to be operative in the teaching and learning of practice.

Supervision Principles

Our study has described the experience supervisors and interns had of supervision;

the perceptions they had of themselves and their roles during the year of supervision; and the metaphors they used to organize their thinking about ministry during that same year. These three analyses present a coherent picture of each of the four individuals studied. They reveal the journey of each intern into the world of the practice of urban ministry, and they show how supervisors involved themselves in those journeys.

We have chosen to view the pattern of the relationships between supervisor and intern, as well as the journey of each member of the team. That pattern is quite different for each dyad. We are convinced that the relationship between supervisor and intern, itself, developed over time so that through supervision there is the generation of a dyad. The development of a relationship does not always occur, even when people work or live together over long periods of time. We submit, however, that such development is required in the teaching and learning of practice. The reason for this is that practice involves personal acts constructed in response to the specific needs of other persons. Although it employs techniques, it cannot be reduced to these. It is learned as it is experienced and as it is done. The investment of one person in another entails negotiations and commitments that build over time. For practice to be taught and learned, the persons of the supervisor and intern must engage.

There are four principles that have surfaced for us in our study of the supervision dyads, which govern the teaching and learning of practice there. They deal with the persons involved (principles of match and mutuality); with the context (principle of task); and with the use of time (principle of recursion).

PRINCIPLE OF MATCH

The worlds from which partners in supervision come are important. It is not that these "preunderstandings" must agree. It is, rather, that their existence must be acknowledged. If the partners in supervision do not distinguish themselves from one another, there is no partnership, and little prospect for the generation of a teaching-learning relationship.

The process required to establish a match is "role taking." John H. Flavell (The Development of Role-Taking and Communication Skills in Children. New York: John Wiley and Sons, 1968) distinguishes this from "role playing," insisting that it involves a transfer from one's own perspective to the perceptual frame of another. Martin Buber (Between Man and Man. Boston: Beacon, 1947) simply calls it "crossing over."

Matching does not happen just at the beginning of a relationship, or only once. It is the result of an orientation toward another person. The match rests in the acknowledgement of another's difference from oneself.

S-1 and I-1 revealed considerable Match during the year. S-1 knew about and drew on the considerable experience I-1 brought with marginal youth in prison systems. At the same time, S-1 acknowledged his own skills as an experienced urban pastor - a world I-1 had not yet entered.

I-1 began with less ability to Match. He felt the need, initially, to populate the entire scope of parish life with the metaphors for ministry he brought from the juvenile justice system. It was only after his response strategies failed that he began to see the validity and power of his partner's alternative "world."

S-2 and I-2 never did "role take" with one another. The absorption of each in her/his own world appears in all analyses. They did not come to function as partners. They engaged one another using static role concepts: as hired help or object of ministry or simply as friend. The world of each developed in many ways through the year, but not in partnership with the world of the other.

PRINCIPLE OF MUTUALITY

The acknowledgement of the world of another may develop into an engaging of that world. The result can be an indwelling (Cf. Michael Polanyi and Harry Prosch, Meaning. Chicago: The University of Chicago Press, 1975). Mutuality has to do with giving and receiving. For Erik H. Erikson mutuality labels a reciprocity involving the exchange of strengths and needs (Insight and Responsibility. New York: Norton, 1964). For Wayne R. Rood it labels the essential relationship of personal teaching and learning (On Nurturing

Christians. New York: Abingdon, 1972).

Mutuality refers to the activity through which relationship is generated. It begins with the recognition of difference and limit. It proceeds as partners reveal their needs and offer their strengths to one another, simultaneously. The key to the activity of mutuality is the reciprocal balancing of the expression of vulnerability and the offering of aid. The result is risk taking and caring between partners.

Both I-1 and I-2 entered supervision intent on communicating their strengths. During the fall, each sought "to minister" to their supervisor. S-1 responded to these overtures by revealing his own deep and authentic needs. He thereby set a social context within which I-1 could confess and explore his own experiences of limitation and failure. The mutual confession of needs destabilized the conventional pattern each person used to defend his professional response. The result was painful, but opened opportunities for both persons to reconceptualize their responses and their understandings of ministry. S-1 could now join his congregation in mourning the death of its members - a participation that goes beyond the role of "comforter." And I-1 could walk the streets to seek reconciliation with his youth - a participation that goes beyond the role of "teacher."

S-2 declined to make his own needs a point of supervisorial exchange. This refusal, expressed as a requirement of institutional good order, became, ironically, a focal point for the relationship between S-2 and I-2. I-2 insisted that S-2 had isolated himself at his work to the point that he "needed" her ministerial attention. Supervision came to be a political jockeying in which she persevered in her intent, and he persevered in deflecting it. Little was done to address the circumstances of and response to their "street congregation." Their interchange was mediated through "a war of words." I-2 fought with religious language, including prayer. S-2 fought with the language of political and institutional organization. Each used concepts and ideas to protect and distance themselves from the other, and from tasks they shared.

PRINCIPLE OF TASK

On the surface, S-2 and I-2 appeared more "task oriented" than did S-1 and I-1. S-2 and I-2 wrote logs about the organization of the center, their roles in it, a "theology for the street." On the other hand, S-1 and I-1 wrote logs about the pain in their congregation, their feelings of elation and failure, their efforts to stabilize themselves as they poised themselves to respond to their people.

Sociologists discriminate between "task functions" and "maintenance functions" (Talcott Parsons and R. Bales, Family Socialization and Interaction Process. New York: The Free Press of Glencoe, 1955). Task functions deal with more objective matters - activities which get the job done. Maintenance functions deal with more personal matters - activities which keep the actors going. In this way of thinking, S-2 sought to supervise task functions - how to administer an agency in the midst of both political and ideological turmoil. S-1, on the other hand, sought to supervise maintenance functions - how to survive, personally, in the midst of pain and the sense of failure.

We have come to the conclusion that Task refers, not to a characterization of what is to be done, but to the "ground" on which the parties in supervision meet. It has to do less with an "espoused" agenda; it has more to do with the "agenda in practice" (Cf. Chris Argyris and Donald A. Schoen, Theory in Practice: Increasing Professional Effectiveness. San Francisco: Jossey-Bass, 1974.) Adam Curle argues that significant interchange in cross-cultural consultation occurs within the context of a common task (Educational Planning: The Adviser's Role. Paris: UNESCO: International Institute for Educational Planning, 1968). Consultants, he says, should not simply talk about problems with their hosts; they should work together.

We believe that supervision can constitute an act of ministry. In it a professional practice can happen. Professional practice is taught and learned by doing and experiencing it. As Schoen insists (Educating the Reflective Practitioner. San Francisco: Jossey-Bass, 1987), supervision for reflective practice requires both professional action and critical reflection on it. Supervision is not complete when it is limited to talk about practice. Supervision requires the work of practice - right there - as the context for talk.

The task of supervision will vary from profession to profession. Schoen illustrates several options (<u>Educating the Reflective Practitioner</u>). The studio master architect draws; the maestro plays an instrument. There, is, to be sure, "talk about." But it refers to what is happening <u>now</u>, in the exchange between teacher and learner. Adam Curle's consultant brings formal, technical knowledge - but it is put forward to inform the problem at hand.

Ministry of presence has to do with remaining <u>in situ</u>, both physically and psychologically, with the people one serves. The ministerial supervisor seeks, in the first place, to do this with the intern. It is within this practice that teaching talk (reflection) is done. S-1 sought to practice presence by making the supervision setting congruent with the "world" of ministry he shared with I-1 - uncertain, vulnerable, full of pain. He brought these human realities into the session himself-- and he stayed there with them. Supervision was not a "release" from daily work - it was part of it.

For S-2, supervision required finding a time "to get away." It could happen in the chinks between professional activity. It had to give way when the demands of professional activity were too great. I-2 was, for S-2, a free supplementary resource - not integral to his professional practice. He would be glad to talk to her about his work, if there were time and if she had interest. The frame for their conversation was theoretical language - "language games" - not personal presence. The practice supervised was a form of political practice, not a ministry of presence.

PRINCIPLE OF RECURSION

When teaching and learning is presumed to occur through "reflection-in-action," its basic rhythms differ from those of most traditional schooling. Most schooling is organized to provide instruction on theory, to be applied at a future date to practice. The procedure is to abstract principles from practice to be taught in classrooms. The transition from the conceptual organization of classroom material to the interactive experience of practice is either assumed or left for "field education." The results, historically, have not been satisfying.

The teaching and learning of practice is better conceptualized as a recursive process in which reflection surfaces again and again within the flow of practice. The process assumes a series of loops between thought and action, each of which builds on the information and experience gained from the prior loop. In this structure, both teacher and learner remain immersed in the practice context and, simultaneously, design and assess that process using skills of reflection. Where practice is the purpose of teaching and learning, there will be no end to the process of recursion. The assessment done in this context is always formative, leading to the next instance of professional practice.

S-1 and I-1 met weekly for supervision. S-1 began the year with considerable felt pressure to use the time to clear and settle program matters. He resisted this tendency in favor of the personal core of the practice of ministry, making interaction between him and I-1 basic to their reflection. The task of supervision deepened from talk about program planning to the practice of being present to one another. This was interpreted to be a sample of the professional practice in which each engaged outside supervision. The relationship itself, as a sample of ministry, became an appropriate task around which to do and experience professional practice. It became a continuity of their interaction, permitting them to design and assess it recursively. S-1 revealed his growing awareness of this process of recursive development by reporting his need to review last week's supervision prior to each current session; by insisting on time for prayer and meditation to ready <u>himself</u> for his practice during the session; and by arranging for one basic interactive theme to focus the several superivison sessions each month. These redundancies were experienced both by him and by I-1 as powerful maneuvers for building competence in practice.

S-2 and I-2 did not establish the regularities for recursive learning. They met and wrote logs irregularly. Since the task had become a rational one, supervision took shape around the topic they agreed on each time as the arena for their "language game." During the spring, they too adopted a monthly theme. Whereas S-1 and I-1 chose to focus on the recognition and acknowledgement of personal gifts, S-2 and I-2 chose the more rational focus of "a theology of the street." They found a number of rational gambits to demonstrate their differences from one another. The result could not be called recursive.

* * * * *

We have identified four principles which we believe pertain to the relationship of supervision, where teaching and learning practice is the schooling goal. The first two reveal the core of the relationship to be personal. It is interaction which contains information - rather than information about interaction (Cf. Paul Watzlawick, Janet H. Beavin and Don D. Jackson, Pragmatics of Human Communication. New York: Norton, 1967). Supervision for practice requires each party to acknowledge the difference of the other (principle of match) and to engage personally with the other's world (principle of mutuality). Such supervision proceeds through the execution of tasks appropriate to professional practice, thereby permitting both the doing and experiencing of practice as the foundation of the relationship (principle of task). Finally, supervision for practice proceeds over time, with reflection in action, which assesses what has been experienced in supervision and its analogs outside supervision, and designs responses that build on the assessment (principle of recursion).

Consultation Principles

Beyond the supervision relationship, our study has focussed on the consultation relationship between each member of the supervision team and the writer of feedback on their logs. The point of this relationship is to promote the mastery of "practice" in a generalizable, public form. Michael Polanyi reminds us that "we know more than we can say" (The Tacit Dimension. Garden City, N.Y.: Doubleday, 1966). The teaching and learning of practice stretches traditional schooling in its efforts to deal with that "more" through contextual and interactive arrangements. The principles of supervision propose "acknowledgement," "engagement," "common action ground," "formative assessment." All of these admit verbal formulation, but none is epistemically exhausted by it. To the extent that practice needs to reflect a community and a tradition, it needs language so that its thrust and process can be recognized and affirmed by a community of reference - a public. In ministry, the community of reference is the church, and the language distinctive to that community is theological language.

The consultation relationship supports the teaching and learning of practice by tutoring the supervision dyad in the acquisition, formation and use of concepts through which to understand practice in communally approved ways. The concept training sought is complicated in the way Vygotsky has suggested. What is sought is more than the verbal mastery by team members of the technical language of the guild (though these have their use and are relatively easy to teach and learn). What is sought is community understood language to designate experiences with which practice deals - language which is more difficult to learn because it formulates an experience which always has more to it than can be said.

Language training for teaching and learning practice is mediated, we believe, by a "scholar/teacher" - a role attempted by the writer of log feedback in our project. Both parts of this role are important. As scholar, the consultant is responsible to know and use the language of some discipline (public) in a clearly recognizable way. In our project the scholar needed to use language theologically - in ways that connect with the tradition and experience of the church.

As teacher, the consultant is responsible to respond to the efforts team members made to formulate practice. The teaching task is not to lay out the technical conceptual scheme of a discipline, which the teacher has mastered. The task is to assist team members to form and use concepts around their practice which bind them to their publics. Our study sought to learn where and how such language learning could occur.

We have concluded that the writing of logs and log feedbacks may promote concept acquisition, formation and use which is appropriate to teaching and learning practice. Our study shows that there is a specific and limited use of speech acts in this interchange, and that the interaction itself occurs through role specific behavior. Our research has not specified or tested the details of language and role in the consultation relationship. In fact, they may be complex in ways that do not permit much precision. We have, however, derived three principles from our study of the feedback dyads which we believe to be important to teaching and learning practice. They deal with the translation of experience into language (principle of reflection training); with the impact of the log-feedback relationship (principle of interrupting response); and with the structure of feedback (principle of conceptual play).

PRINCIPLE OF REFLECTION TRAINING

The consultation relationship deals with the acquisition, formation and use of concepts. The material with which it works is linguistic. It seeks to transform experience into language through which to think, design and communicate practice.

The log exercizes pressed for a verbalization of experience in two ways that promoted reflection. First, the structure of the log required the generation of speech acts that gathered the log writer's observation and presumptions into a single artifact. The log invited the writer to select something that happened, report it, and assign meaning to it. The log structure required that the assignment of meaning be done with an eye to future practice. The linking of observation and meaning is at the heart of reflection. It requires a classification of activity - a rendering of the form of an event.

Log writers had difficulty doing what the log structure requested. Training in reflection required repeated efforts. The repetition gave an opportunity not only for refining logging skills; it also established a rhythm of action and reflection, reinforcing the "future practice" bias of the logging exercize. In fact, the recursive aspect of log reflection followed the mastery of log writing skills. Until log writers learned to select, report and assign meaning, it was not possible for them effectively to reflect within the flow of their practice. Concepts could not be formed from their practice until they were able to describe and evaluate their practice themselves.

PRINCIPLE OF INTERRUPTING RESPONSE

The consultation relationship introduces a meta-relationship to support the primary, intimate supervision relationship through which practice is taught and learned. Intimacy brings with it a variety of pressures to develop idiosyncratic communication. Sometimes we know people so well that we "converse" with them using shorthand that mystifies everyone else. This is the result of investment in one another, and in the particular "world version" brought by one's partner.

For practice to be effective, it must communicate to a community of reference. Log feedback, written by a representative of that community outside the supervision dyad promotes such broader accountability. It was easy for S-1 and I-1 to share the pain and failure they felt in their work. Log feedback pressed them to see that pain as characteristic of ministry, as a symbol of redemption, as a reality in the Christian's world view. Feedback interrupted their feelings and proposed conceptual transformations which helped them design role acts (sermons, retreats, pastoral visits) through which practice was done with heightened awareness and skill.

S-2 and I-2 were less interrupted by feedback because their logs matched more directly the conceptual tone which the feedback writer brought. The logs they presented were of their thinking rather than of their feeling. Neither feedback structure nor the feedback writer was adept at interrupting those rational frames. Notwithstanding the apparent rational match, the feedback writer needed to interrupt the logging of these supervision partners, pointing them to the rational _patina_ that covered their efforts to reflect on practice.

The Speech Act Analysis shows differential responses of the feedback writer to log writers by role. This fits what we know of the stimulus value which classes of people have on one another. However the resulting patterns were a surprize to the feedback writer. The feedback response needs to be adjusted to role. The thrust of the principle of interrupting response is that whatever the log writer's role or logging style, the feedback needs to interrupt the log writer's conventional logic and communication form in order to invite a more adequate or more sophisticated selection, report or assignation of meaning, in the light of the language of the community of reference. This intervention requires that the feedback writer exercize clinical skill in the evaluation of the dynamics of the supervision relationship, as revealed in the logs, in addition to the exercise of language skills required by a scholarly discipline.

PRINCIPLE OF CONCEPTUAL PLAY

Teaching and learning practice involves the formulation of concepts which the learner can apply to professional action that make those actions meaningful to the community of reference. The problem is that practice, like other events which persons experience, involves "more than we can say." Concepts, the tools of communication, apply to less complex matters as they become more precise. Concepts which are adequate to the domain of practice will inevitably be imprecise enough so that communication will be an ongoing struggle.

All thought, says Marc Belth, is analogical. (Process of Thinking. N.Y.: David McKay, 1977). The concepts through which practice is communicated certainly will be. The teaching and learning of practice calls for training in the formation and use of conceptual renderings. The search for clarity must be a game which acknowledges the innate mystery of what is to be communicated. This is especially clear in the case of religious language , which language philosopher I.T. Ramsey calls "riotous" (Christian Discourse. London: Oxford University Press, 1965).

The feedback writer draws concepts from the language pool of a discipline, but presents them playfully, encouraging the log writer to tease them until they "mean" in ways that bridge her/his experience and a public. Each successful approximation adds to a repertoire of expressive forms from which to draw in future efforts to think out practice design or communication. No concept will peg an experience completely. That is why play is needed to approach a satisfying "fit."

* * * * * *

The three principles of the consultation relationship reveal the task of the "scholar/teacher" in the teaching and learning of practice. It is an adjunctive role to the supervision relationship. It exists to keep practice within the scope of a community's understanding, while it assumes practice never to be reducible to a single interpretation. The consultation relationship functions linguistically, through a sequence like the log-log feedback sequence of our study. It trains log writers to encode the world of their practice in ways that interrupt their assumptions and yet bridge them creatively with their community of reference. Such training is given using the skills of a disciplinary scholar who is able to elicit conceptual play from the learner. It gives the learner both the tools to gain support from the community and to inovate future practice.

Professional Schooling

There are three proposals for professional schooling which we would like to make as a result of our study of the teaching and learning of practice. Each suggests an adjustment to the structure of the professional school to accomodate the dimension of practice.

1. MAKE PRACTICE A CONTEXT FOR TEACHING AND LEARNING

It is perhaps the medical school that does this most adequately now. The hospital, as well as the classroom, is a context for teaching and learning. "Rounds" gives teacher and student a chance to relate as they serve a patient. And "on call" places students where treatment is required, hopefully with sufficient on site supervision.

Innovative medical schooling chooses not to limit its context to classroom and hospital. Only a minority of cases of illness ever darken a hospital door. The context for teaching and learning medical practice can be extended to include families and schools.

When schooling is extended to include contexts that have a broad social sweep, its institutional character is changed. We are aware of huge changes in medical delivery (cf. Health Maintenance Organizations in the US and "barefoot doctors" in the Peoples' Republic of China). Changes are needed in professional schooling to match new understandings of professional activity.

Theological schooling typically has occurred in a seminary library and classroom, to which has been appended some form of "field education." In most cases, churches provide the field location and the student is given a modest stipend to do work there. The experience is understood to be "educational" when the student meets with church pastor and/or seminary field education director for planning and "theological reflection." The assumption, frequently, is that the student is to apply in the field what has been learned in class, and is to leave the field for reflection on what she/he has learned.

There is considerable conversation about churches as "teaching partners" with seminaries in theological schooling. Too often the partnership rests in financial contributions by church to seminary, or the provision of a low pay job for the seminarian. In a few cases, clergy and laity in the church constitute a community for teaching and learning practice. We have few schooling names for these rare circumstances. They do not affect the location or schedule or roles or budget of a seminary very extensively.

It is not the point of this proposal to replace classroom and library with church as an exclusive teaching and learning place. The proposal is to begin one's thinking about schooling with professional practice. An examination of ministry, for example, will reveal that acts of ministry are not limited to what happens in local churches. Ministry is done to the non- churched, to social structures, even within seminaries. What is done in these places needs to be explored. Opportunities for teaching and learning within these places need to be provided.

Then it becomes possible to think about the resources, such as books, classrooms and faculty, to support such professional schooling.

2. SUPERVISION IS THE BASIC TEACHING/LEARNING RELATIONSHIP

It is those who deliver professional services that can teach professional practice authentically. Such teaching is not accomplished best by removing the practitioner from practice and changing both her location and role to classroom lecturer. Our study suggests the possibility of involving teacher and learner in the teacher's exercise of practice and to reflect on that practice as it is done. This is an energy and time consuming affair. It requires certain redundancies of schedule and reflective product. We believe that preparation for regular meeting/events (like log writing) is essential. Supervisors need to be given permission to do this work. They need to be paid, either in the coin of salary or guild expectation (cf. volunteer faculty at medical schools). Equally important, they need to be trained and supported in this work. Classroom, library and seminary faculty all can play a part here.

3. CONSULTATION IS AN APPROPRIATE ROLE FOR SEMINARY FACULTY VIS A VIS THE TEACHING OF PRACTICE

"Roles," says Guy Benveniste, "are a principal social asset because they give us the ability to cope with the uncertainty of social encounters....But we change roles or define new roles very slowly because trust and mutual expectations of behavior can only be built up over time." (The Politics of Expertise. Berkeley, Ca.: Glendessary Press, 1972).

The role of seminary faculty needs to be adjusted, just as the role of practitioner needs to be adjusted around the teaching and learning of practice. Faculty are not in a place to be the central figures in teaching practice. Their role is to be scholar/teachers. This is a conservative and constructive role. It deals with tradition and with the generation of new understandings and forms of practice. It is rooted in language.

Every profession needs scholars whose business it is to know a literature and a methodology for the assessment and exploration of practice and for the generation of new knowledge. Without this role, the profession would be cut off from a coherent tradition and community. It could not survive. The skills needed for scholarship are fundamentally conceptual - though good scholarship requires clear sight and clinical sensitivity. Nonetheless, concepts, and language to express them, are critical, especially since professions treat matters that are hard to communicate because they can never be reduced entirely to language.

The faculty member is a teacher as well as a scholar. But the faculty member's teaching is not practice; it is in support of practice. The resource from which the faculty member initiates teaching is scholarly competence. The demand of teaching is to build a bridge between the teaching and learning of practice accomplished through the supervision relationship and the world of scholarship the faculty member knows. The faculty teacher must cross over to the "reflection-in-practice" and become adept at thinking about that using scholarly concepts, and making those concepts available for the use of the practice team. This is not primarily a transmissive process (though there will need to be traditional classes maintained, particularly at the introductory level, to introduce concepts to students systematically). This is primarily a consultative process in which the faculty scholar/teacher listens first - then draws on scholarship to help the supervision dyad clarify their practice.

* * * * *

Theological seminaries espouse the need for field sites as part of education for ministry. But the programs which attend to this are marginalized in a number of ways. Most noticeably, "field education" is separated into a department which is then made responsible for the logistics of field job placement. Sometimes it is hard to know whether the placement is for education or simply for work.

The other side of this coin is that faculty are now relieved of involvement in the teaching and learning of practice. They teach only in classrooms (thereby making classroom teaching the primary and often exclusive business of the faculty). Faculty are encouraged to "minister" to students, but this frequently means little more than attending chapel with them, listening to their personal stories, promoting a career in ministry. Sometimes faculty believe that these personal relationships substitute for scholarly discipline. In short, there is a confusion of roles. Faculty are freed to be scholars, but are pressed to minister. This is the natural outcome of the assumption that theological schooling is entirely the province of the seminary.

Faculty need to become language teachers. They have been trained into a concept-based language in order to preserve what the church has and does value, and to teach a new generation of practitioners that language. The power of the language is not in the formulas. The power is, as it always has been, in the success with which language generates thought and meaning. The language empowers and becomes powerful itself as practitioners use it to enhance their practice, and to draw a community together around the values of a tradition.

To be sure, some of the language teaching will be done directly, in classrooms. But importantly, beyond that, language must function in situ - where professional practice happens. The practitioner works by figuring things out. Concepts make this possible. Language is the tool to facilitate the process. Learning practice is, importantly, learning to use language to figure things out. Faculty need to be involved here too.

Too frequently, in theological schooling, practitioners are validated only as they leave the domain of their practice and become "adjunct faculty." The other common contact with the seminary is when practitioners return for continuing education. When the practitioner is asked to be an adjunct faculty, faculty are relieved of encounter with a practitioner, for they relate with the newcomer as one of themselves - an adjunct faculty member - and, as adjunct, a less experienced one than themselves. When the practitioner returns as an advanced professional student, there is sometimes rhetoric that the presence of such a person opens the world of practice to the faculty. However, the return is in the role of "student." The faculty is asked to instruct and grade; not learn from the newcomer. In these ways the interface between faculty and practitioner is qualified.

Professional schooling needs to locate itself in the context of practice; involve experienced practitioners in a major teaching role; delimit the role of professional faculty, emphasizing their responsibility for the mastery of concepts and the teaching of these for use in reflective practice. These are areas we have uncovered as we engaged in careful observation of alternative professional schooling sites. They require further study.

APPENDIX 1

Descriptors given to ACL scale scores. Each descriptor constitutes a "need to..."

	High Scorers	Low Scorers
General Descriptors		
Favorable	Outgoing	Self-deprecating
Unfavorable	Not easily flapped	Pessimistic re. future

	High Scorers	Low Scorers
Specific Descriptors		
Achievement	To do well	To be diffident
Dominance	To be in charge	To lack confidence
Endurance	To do one's job	To be easily distracted/redirected
Order	To be planful	To get quick gratification
Intraception	To be reflective	To cope with stress
Nurturance	To help others	To be wary of close ties with others
Affiliation	To relate to others	To agonize over the meaning of relations with others
Heterosexuality	To relate to others	To keep people at a distance
Exhibition	To get others' attention	To avoid interpersonal stress
Autonomy	To act independently	To avoid risks
Aggression	To be assertive	To avoid conflict
Change	To avoid routine	To seek stability
Succorance	To solicit emotional support from others	To be unbothered by self doubt
Abasement	To submit to others' wishes	To get one's due
Deference	To take others into account	To take risks

APPENDIX 2

The tables which follow organize the items which received scale scores one standard deviation (10 points) or more above or below the mean (50). Few of the scores qualify for statistical significance at p<.05, since 2.96 standard deviations are required to reach that level. However, we believe that, especially in the light of the conservative nature of the instrument, it is interesting to report deviations from the norm that exceed one standard deviation. We have called such deviations "shifts." The higher/lower the numbers beyond 60/40, the greater the shift. Profiles are given using higher scores first, then lower scores, with the largest shifts reported first in each category.

Supervisor One's (S-1) ACL Scores
diff. from norm =>10

SELF

Fall	Winter	Spring
Fav 60	Fav 64	Fav 70
Nur 64	Nur 61	Nur 74
Aff 66	Aff 60	Aff 74
Het 67	Het 67	Het 76
Def 60		
	Aut 40	
		Ach 62
		Dom 71
		Int 65
		Aba 38

Fall profile: S-1 perceives himself to need to relate to others, to help others, to take others into account. He sees himself as outgoing.

Winter profile: S-1 perceives himself to need to relate to others, to help others, to avoid risk. He sees himself as outgoing.

Spring profile: S-1 perceives himself to need to relate to others, to help others, to be in charge, to reflect, to do well, and to get his due. He sees himself as outgoing.

Supervisor One's (S-1) ACL Scores
diff. from norm =>10

MINISTER TO YOUTH

Fall	Winter	Spring
Fav 67		
Unf 39	Unf 39	
Dom 62		Dom 65
Nur 63		Nur 63
Aff 63		
Het 67		Het 68
Exh 60		
	End 65	End 60
		Ach 65
		Suc 39
		Aba 38

Fall profile: S-1 perceives ministers to youth to need to relate to others, to help others, to be in charge, to get others' attention. He sees such ministers to be outgoing and not easily flapped.

Winter profile: S-1 perceives ministers to youth to need to do their job. He sees such ministers as not easily flapped.

Spring profile: S-1 perceives ministers to youth to need to relate to others, to be in charge, to do well, to help others, to do their job, to get their due, to be unbothered by self doubt.

Supervisor One's (S-1) ACL Scores
diff. from norm =>10

<u>YOUTH YOU SERVE</u>

Fall	Winter	Spring
Fav 14	Fav 20	Fav 27
Unf 96	Unf 96	Unf 85
Ach 26	Ach 35	Ach 32
End 19	End 21	End 26
Ord 19	Ord 20	Ord 22
Int 2	Int 21	Int 24
Nur 19	Nur 24	Nur 23
Aff 26	Aff 30	Aff 36
Exh 71	Exh 66	Exh 60
Aut 70	Aut 73	Aut 62
Agg 75	Agg 72	Agg 68
Cha 70	Cha 67	
Suc 76	Suc 73	Suc 73
Def 24	Def 29	Def 32

Fall profile: S-1 perceives the youth he serves to need to solicit emotional support from others, to be assertive, to get others' attention, to act independently, to avoid routine, to cope with stress, to be easily distracted/redirected, to be wary of close ties with others, to get quick gratification, to take risks, to agonize over the meaning of relations with others, to be diffident. He sees them as self-deprecating and pessimistic about the future.

Winter profile: S-1 perceives the youth he serves to need to solicit emotional support from others, to act independently, to be assertive, to avoid routine, to get others' attention, to get quick gratification, to cope with stress, to be easily distracted/redirected, to be wary of close ties with others, to take risks, to agonize over the meaning of relations with others, to be diffident. He sees them as self-deprecating and pessimistic about the future.

Spring profile: S-1 perceives the youth he serves to need to solicit emotional support from others, to be assertive, to act independently, to get others' attention, to get quick gratification, to be wary of close ties with others, to cope with stress, to be easily distracted/redirected, to take risks, to agonize over the meaning of relationships with others. He sees them as self-deprecating and pessimistic about the future.

Intern One"s (I-1) ACL Scores
diff. from norm =>10

<u>SELF</u>

Fall	Winter	Spring
Dom 67	Dom 60	
Aff 62		
Het 61		Het 69
	Aba 39	
		Unf 39
		End 61
		Nur 60

Fall profile: I-1 perceives himself to need to be in charge and to relate to others.

Winter profile: I-1 perceives himself to need to be in charge and to get his due.

Spring profile: I-1 perceives himself to need to relate to others, to do his job, to help others. He sees himself as not easily flapped.

Intern One's (I-1) ACL Scores
diff. from norm =>10

<u>MINISTER TO YOUTH</u>

Fall	Winter	Spring
Fav 72		Fav 64
Unf 39		Unf 39
Ach 61		
Dom 62		
End 64		
Int 60		Int 61
Nur 70		
Aff 67		
Het 67		Het 67
Exh 60		
Suc 39	Suc 34	

Fall profile: I-1 perceives ministers to youth to need to help others, to relate to others, to do their job, to be in charge, to do well, to get others' attention, to reflect to be unbothered by self doubt. He sees such ministers to be outgoing and not easily flapped.

Winter profile: I-1 perceives ministers to youth to need to be unbothered by self doubt.

Spring profile: I-1 perceives ministers to youth to need to relate to others and to reflect. He sees such ministers to be outgoing and not easily flapped.

Intern one"s (I-1) ACL Scores
diff. from norm =>10

<u>YOUTH YOU SERVE</u>

Fall	Winter	Spring
Ord 39	Ord 36	
Int 38	Int 33	Int 63
Het 61	Het 64	Het 75
Exh 62	Exh 60	
Aut 67		
Agg 64		
Aba 37	Aba 61	
	Fav 36	Fav 64
	Unf 71	Unf 39
	Nur 39	
	Suc 63	
		Aff 60

Fall profile: I-1 perceives youth he serves to need to act independently, to be assertive, to get others' attention, to relate to others, to get their due, to cope with stress, to get quick gratification.

Winter profile: I-1 perceives youth he serves to need to relate to others, to solicit emotional support from others, to submit to others' wishes, to get others' attention, to cope with stress, to get quick gratification, to be wary of close ties with others. He sees them as self deprecating and pessimistic about the future.

Spring profile: I-1 perceives youth he serves to need to relate to others, and to reflect. He sees them as outgoing and not easily flapped.

50

Supervisor Two's (S-2) ACL Scores
diff. from norm =>10

<u>SELF</u>

Fall	Winter	Spring
Nur 39		
Aut 63	Aut 63	Aut 62
Def 37		
Exh 60		
Agg 63	Agg 63	
Aba 38		
	Ach 65	
	Dom 65	
	Aff 38	
		Cha 60

Fall profile: S-2 perceives himself to need to act independently, to be assertive, to get others' attention, to take risks, to get his due, to be wary of close dies with others.

Winter profile: S-2 perceives himself to need to be in charge, to do well, to act independently, to be assertive, to agonize over the meaning of relations with others.

Spring profile: S-2 perceives himself to need to act independently, to avoid routine, to take risks.

Supervisor Two's (S-2) ACL Scores
diff. from norm =>10

<u>MINISTER TO YOUTH</u>

Fall	Winter	Spring
Fav 68	Fav 61	Fav 62
Unf 39		
Dom 62	Dom 61	Dom 65
Int 65	Int 65	Int 68
	Ord 36	
	Nur 63	
	Aff 60	Aff 63
	Exh 60	
	Cha 67	Cha 60
		End 60
		Suc 39
		Aba 38

Fall profile: S-2 perceives ministers to youth to need to reflect and to be in charge. He sees them as outgoing and not easily flapped.

Winter profile: S-2 perceives ministers to youth to need to avoid routine, to reflect, to help others, to be in charge, to relate to others, to get others' attention, to get quick gratification. He sees them as outgoing.

Spring profile: S-2 perceives ministers to youth to need to reflect, to be in charge, to relate to others, to avoid routine, to do their job, to get their due, to be unbothered by self doubt. He sees them as outgoing.

YOUTH YOU SERVE

Fall	Winter	Spring
Fav 23	Fav 19	Fav 40
Unf 64	Unf 75	
End 35	End 28	End 29
Ord 33	Ord 20	Ord 22
Int 17	Int 17	Int 36
Nur 26	Nur 21	
Aff 32	Aff 24	
Exh 64		
Aut 62	Aut 67	Aut 63
Agg 70	Agg 67	
Def 27	Def 32	Def 28
	Ach 35	
	Het 40	
	Suc 62	Suc 63
	Aba 61	Aba 64
		Cha 71

Fall profile: S-2 perceives the youth he serves to need to be assertive, to get others' attention, to act independently, to cope with stress, to be wary of close ties with others, to take risks, to agonize over the meaning of relations with others, to get quick gratification, to be easily distracted/redirected. He sees them as self deprecating and pessimistic about the future.

Winter profile: S-2 perceives the youth he serves to need to be assertive, to act independently, to solicit emotional support from others, to submit to others' wishes, to cope with stress, to get quick gratification, to be wary of close ties with others, to agonize over the meaning of relations with others, to be easily distracted/redirected, to take risks, to be diffident, to keep people at a distance. He sees them as self deprecating and pessimistic about the future.

Spring profile: S-2 perceives the youth he serves to need to avoid routine, to submit to others' wishes, to solicit emotional support from others, to act independently, to get quick gratification, to take risks, to be easily distracted/redirected, to cope with stress. He sees them as self deprecating.

Intern Two's (I-2) ACL Scores
diff. from norm =>10

SELF

Fall	Winter	Spring
Fav 62		
Unf 40	Unf 39	Unf 39
Int 63	Int 64	
Aff 63		
	Het 60	
	Aut 39	
	Agg 40	

Fall profile: I-2 perceives herself to need to reflect and to relate to others. She sees herself as outgoing and not easily flapped.

Winter profile: I-2 perceives herself to need to reflect, to relate to others, to avoid risks and conflicts. She sees herself as not easily flapped.

Spring profile: I-2 perceives herself as not easily flapped.

Intern Two's (I-2) ACL Scores
diff. from norm =>10

MINISTER TO YOUTH

Fall	Winter	Spring
Fav. 60	Fav 60	
	Int 67	
	Nur 63	
	Aff 66	Aff 62
	Cha 62	

Fall profile: I-2 perceives ministers to youth as outgoing.

Winter profile: I-2 perceives ministers to youth to need to be reflective, to relate to others, to help others, to avoid routine. She sees them as outgoing.

Spring profile: I-2 perceives ministers to youth to need to relate to others.

Intern Two's (I-2) ACL Scores
diff. from norm =>10

YOUTH YOU SERVE

Fall	Winter	Spring
Fav 31	Fav 34	Fav 40
Unf 60	Unf 64	
End 39	End 21	End 31
Ord 39	Ord 27	Ord 32
Int 31	Int 24	Int 24
Nur 31	Nur 38	
Aff 38		
Exh 60	Exh 66	Exh 67
Aut 64	Aut 71	Aut 61
Agg 65		Agg 62
Suc 34	Suc 64	
Def 39	Def 32	Def 33
	Dom 40	
	Cha 74	Cha 69
		Het 65
		Aba 40

Fall profile: I-2 perceives the youth she serves to need to be assertive, to act independently, to get others' attention, to cope with stress, to be wary of close ties with others, to be unbothered by self doubt, to agonize over the meaning of relations with others, to be easily distracted/redirected, to get quick gratification, to take risks. She sees them as self deprecating and pessimistic about the future.

Winter profile: I-2 perceives the youth she serves to need to avoid routine, to act independently, to get others' attention, to solicit emotional support from others, to be easily distracted/redirected, to cope with stress, to get quick gratification, to take risks, to be wary of close ties with others, to lack confidence. She sees them as self deprecating and pessimistic about the future.

Spring profile: I-2 perceives the youth she serves to need to avoid routine, to get others' attention, to relate to others, to be assertive, to act independently, to cope with stress, to be easily distracted/redirected, to get quick gratification, to take risks, to get their due. She sees them as self deprecating.

APPENDIX 3

Dominant Metaphors for Ministry

Derived from autobiographies, logs, interviews of team members

* * * * *

MINISTER AS PARENT

Parents provide for children
Parents care for children
Parents discipline children
Parents protect children
Parents love children
Parents nurture children
Parents teach children important cultural and social
    norms
Parents play with children
Parents model how emotions and difficult situations
    are handled
Parents mediate conflicts
Parents introduce children into the institutions
    of society and mediate between the
    institutions and children
Parents alleviate children's fears
Parents encourage children
Parents express their expectations of children
Parents help children achieve their sense of selfhood

MINISTER AS TEACHER

Teachers are authorities in subject areas
Teachers impart their knowledge to children and
    adults who do not have this knowledge
Teachers' authority is based upon experience
Teachers are a source of wisdom
Teachers direct thoughts/thinking
Teachers present "facts" of the social, cultural world
Teachers are able to impart certain skills

MINISTER AS AGENT

Agents stimulate the actions of others
Agents have a social awareness which what needs to
    be done
Agents are persuasive
Agents work on behalf of others
Agents set policy
Agents guide activity/lead
Agents coordinate activities
Agents have sanctioned or acknowledged authority
Agents announce plans of actions

MINISTER AS PRIEST

Priests are identified by a social structure to
    perform certain rituals or roles
Priests are identified by certain activities,
    manners, symbols, styles
Priests have moral authority
Priests have the knowledge necessary to carry their
    roles
Priests lead people
Priests mediate between worlds
Priests command respect

MINISTER AS HELPER

Helpers have some skill or gift which can be utilized
    to improve the situation of another
Helpers use their influence or skill to accomplish
    work
Helpers "fill gaps" in various activities or in
    people's lives
Helpers render a service
Helpers lend their skills/gifts to others so that
    the other may accomplish something else

MINISTER AS SAVIOR

Saviors possess a power or strength to rescue others
    from impossible situations
Saviors can eliminate or overcome dangerous situations
Saviors have basic skills or attitudes which
    they offer to rescue others
Saviors are able to perceive the peril of a situation
    and save others from it
Saviors are always successful in averting disasters

MINISTER AS HEALER

Healers perceive sickness or injury
Healers eradicates
Healers restore sick or injured persons to wholeness
    unity and/or health
Healers use the power found in the injured or sick
    person to restore the person to wholeness/health

MINISTER AS COMMUNICATOR

Communicators talk or gesture to others their
    intentions, desires, thoughts, feelings,
    perceptions
Communicators listen to the "talk" of others and
    respond as appropriate
Communicators mediate their internal world of
    experience to the external world shared by
    the listener

MINISTER AS TRANSLATOR

Translators relate the knowledge of one language
    or symbolic system to another
Translators are intermediaries between systems
Translators give people of different experiences
    access to each others symbol systems
Translators can make the unknown or incompre-
    hensible aspects of one experience
    understandable to an individual

MINISTER AS COUNSELOR

Counselors listen to the problems of others
Counselors are educated in the feeling side
    of human experience
Counselors recognize the importance of feelings
    in human experience
Counselors offer solutions to feeling problems
    as necessary
Counselors encourage a person to find his/her
    own solution to problems
Counselors share the feeling experiences of
    others
Counselors are empathetic
Counselors are supportive
Counselors are accepting

MINISTER AS WITNESS

Witnesses have chosen a particular way of living
Witnesses display this way of living in daily
        life
Witnesses desire others to choose this way of
        living
Witnesses attempt to entice or persuade others
        to live in a similar way
Witnesses attempt to show certain subtleties about
        life which give meaning
Witnesses attempt to bring people to "faith"
        revealed in their way of life

MINISTER AS JESUS CHRIST

Jesus healed the sick and injured
Jesus offered acceptance and love to all
Jesus gently called sinners to repentance
Jesus' presence had a healing or nurturing effect
        on those encountered
Jesus brought God's grace to people he encountered
Jesus knew the power and presence of God in his
        own life
Jesus confronted the powers and suffered

MINISTER AS FRIEND

Friends care for those they love
Friends are present in times of trouble and joy
Friends listen to problems and difficulties
Friends share with each other their hidden selves
Friends trust each other
Friends are loyal
Friends are honest

MINISTER AS WOUNDED OR WEAK PERSON

Wounded/weak people are limited in the range of
        activities they can pursue
Wounded/weak people know their limitations
Wounded/weak people are vulnerable to various
        external dangers
Wounded/weak people must rely on others for help
Wounded/weak people must be protected/cared for by
        others
Wounded/weak people must trust others
Wounded/weak people must allows others to help if
        they are so survive

MINISTER AS SERVANT

Servants are at the beckon call of others
Servants have little choice about what they
        may do
Servants are dependent upon others for orders
Servants are identified only by what they do
Servants' tasks are determined by others

MINISTER AS NAMER

Namers make order out of chaos by identifying
        patterns or designs and applying words to
        them
Namers live in the midst of disorder and make
        order from it through the power of naming
Namers have power
Namers have insight
Namers have intuition
Namers provide a means for others to act in the
        newly found order

MINISTER AS ROLE

>Roles are sanctioned by a culture or social order
>Roles are recognized in the performance of certain
>   actions
>Roles require certain manners, symbols, style
>Roles are well defined
>Roles are identified through activities/actions

MINISTER AS ENTITY

>Entities have boundaries
>Entities have identifiable characteristics
>Entities are contained or are containable
>Entities are objects/things
>Entities have identifiable location
>Entities have identifiable positions in space/time/
>   world
>Entities can do things

MINISTER AS PERSONA

>Personaes present a face to the public with certain
>   characteristics and qualities
>Personaes act in limited ways which but in ways
>   which can be shaped the temperment of the actors
>   and demands of the situation
>Personaes reveal certains aspects of their person
>   but not all

APPENDIX 4

Guidelines for Content Analysis

* * * * *

The following guidelines were developed from Fall written material and were used to review Spring log and log feedback material.

1a) Opening greeting
1b) Setting context for following comments

2)   Instructional use of log

3)   Restating of log writer's comment

4)   Support or encouragement given by log reader

5)   Interesting grammar and stylistic features

6)   Identification markers
>   a) I
>   b) me
>   c) you
>   d) we (group of persons apart from participant)
>   e) us (group of persons apart from participant)
>   f) WE (group of persons including participant)
>   g) US (group of persons including participant)

7)   Elaborations of themes presented in log or by reader
>   - Statements usually made in the third person,
>   generalized "we," or stated in the impersonal
>   mode.
>   - Statements which explain, expand, support,
>   clarify Assertions, Interpretations, Conjectures.
>   - Statements which are not generally topic
>   sentences - unless statement clearly continues
>   thought of previous paragraph.

- Statements which generally report known facts, common knowledge, but set in new contexts and relationships.
- Statements may or may not solicit responses from reader.

8) Reader's value statement
- Statements which usually begin "I believe," "I value."
- Statements which emphasize something of importance to the writer.
- Statements which may serve as elaborations.
- Statements which make strong assertions.
-Statements which appear to have justification or validation apart from the immediate context or location.

9) Questions posed
    a) Clarification or requesting more information.
    b) Challenging or probing.
    c) Musing.
    d) Checking comments.

10) Name usage

11) Closing comments

12) Explanation of some procedures

13) Explanation or internal moves within the discourse

14) Conjecture statements
- Statements made in the subjunctive mood.
- Statements using modals (may, might, could, perhaps, etc.)
- Statements beginning "My guess is..."
- Statements which make tentative or weak assertions.
- Statements which make tentative interpretations.
- Statements which are cloaked directives.
- Statements which invite correction, argument, disagreement, or agreement from reader.
- Statement which pose a possible line of action or world rendering.

15) Interpretative statements
- Statements which begin "I take it..." "I understand..." "What I hear you saying..."
- Statements which "read between the lines" of a given text-- piece together connections or pieces of evidence.
- Statements drawn from a description statement.
- Statements which invite responses of correction, argument, reinterpretation.
- Statements which may require elaboration to show how the interpretation was formed.

16) Description from logs
- Statements which quote, restate, reassert, narrate what has appeared in the log text.
-Statements which report what has happened in other logs or feedback responses.
- Statements which do not generally call for response from the reader.

17) Reader's assertions
- Statements which usually begin "I think..." "I find..." "I hope...." "I want..."

- Statements which imply "I think" "I find" "I
hope" "I weant."
- Statement which express the writer's unique
point of view -- writer's rendering of the
situation/world.
- Statements which promise, bet, surmise, etc.,
the truth of a position, conjecture,
interpretation.
- Statements which present a rendering of the
world believed to be true.
- Statements which engage other "renderings of the
world:" demand agreement, disagreement, argument,
correction from reader.
- Statements whose force is illocutionary.
- Statements which provide situations for asking
challenging and checking questions.

18) Parenthetic comments

19) Critique of logs

20) Directives
- Statements with overt or subtle perlocutionary
force
- Statements which are in the imperative mood or
are an implied imperative.
- Statements in the form "Please see...'s log"
"You might want to..." "Don't forget..."
- Statements which are strong assertions directed
toward a specific action.

21) "Thank you" usage

22) Quotations from logs

23) Narratives
- Statements or episodes drawn from writer's
personal experience (apart from log material).
- Statements which serve as elaboration.

APPENDIX 5
EXAMPLES OF LOGS AND FEEDBACK VERBATA

Examples of logs and feedback are reproduced here to give a
flavor of the flow of language used in the log/log feedback
interaction. One log and feedback is given for each supervisor
and intern.

* * * * *

LOG 3: Intern One

Goal: To share my values without disrespecting those of the
community.
Activity: By sharing my history.
Report: I shared with S/1 that on Saturday when I took a group of
youngsters and adults on a field trip, my values came
in sharp contrast to those of the youth.
Their value system involved sharing _after_ individual
satisfaction while mine centered around communal
sharing with each person having a right to equal
participation.
S/1 suggested that I provide structure, share my history,
bring youth into participation in the structure through
the sharing of leadership role and then discuss with
them what it feels like to be part of a communal
situation.
Learning: How painful conflict can be.
That youth need the structure they rebel against.
Evaluation: I will share myhistory with youth.

Feedback
Sharing one's own values without disrespecting community values
    is a good follow-up to the last log.
I think your strategy of sharing your history is just the way to
    do it.
I remember the humanistic psychologists who remind us to talk
    about controversial matters using "I" statements.
One should say, "This is the way I see it" rather than "This is
    the way everyone should see it."

I don't quite understand what you mean by "Their value system
    involved sharing _after_ individual satisfaction...."
I think I find an issue of absence of loyalty to the community,
    but perhaps you could say a bit more about this in the
    interview.
A bit more will help me understand the suggestions S/1 made to
    you.

LOG 3:   Supervisor One

Goal: To identify and affirm persons' gifts in ministry
Activity: In the supervisory session I listen to the energy behind
            I/1's words to discover the focus for identifying and
            affirming gifts in ministry.
Report: During supervision this week, I/1 reported on an outing
            last week with some parishioners and children from
            the housing project.
        At the beginning of the described event -- a trip to the
            police stables and picnic following -- he began
            by saying that the first half of the afternoon's
            event went very well, but in the second half, he
            could not "tolerate" the kids.
        I noted that to myself and listened for what was intolerable
            about the experience.
        In conversation I pressed for a better understanding of the
            sources within him that was termed a "conflict of
            values."
        The conversation clarified for I/1 the conflict.
        Through affirming what he had to offer the kids, namely his
            own personal story and the value of structure, we
            identified paths for conflict resolution and his
            own power in ministry.
Learning: Listening intently and listening for "the conflict" is
            key to an effective supervisory hour.
          If I had not listened with "the third ear" I, and he, could
            have let pass unnoticed the true conflict, rather
            than the one he thought he was bringing to
            supervision.
Evaluation: I think I will add a few minutes for summarizing
            learnings at the end of next session.

Feedback

It is just the thing, I think, to listen during the session,
    after you have listened in preparing for the session.
With you, I picked up a gap in I/1's log on conflict of
    values with the kids.
In my log feedback to him, I told him I didn't understand what he
    said about "their value system."
I'm glad you pressed that.
It's not important for me to understand, but it is important for
    I/1 to be clear, and you, I think, are the person to help him
    clarify.
The last sentence of your "Report" is very important, I think.
I/1   frequently takes the position of teacher/parent in his logs.
    He "explains" a lot to his kids.
You are indicating that I/1 sometimes questions what he has
    to offer the kids.
I believe that as he factors his own uncertainties and need for
    grace into his ministry, he (like the rest of us) will grow in
    the power of the Spirit.

I think you're correct that issues like these come up and require response <u>during</u> the supervision session.

LOG 3: Intern Two

Goal: Dialogue -- personal and theological
Activity: Change structure of session. Prayer-honesty-share
Report: Talked, focused on theological concepts
      Discussion was in depth and very thought provoking.
      An understanding of God is possible only in relationship
         with God.
      (Key issue for us)
      God is being.
      Being in relationships with humans - kids, teachers, staff -
         -and God's nature can only be truly known as humans
         submit themselves to <u>intimate relationship</u> with
         God and thereby experience these theological constructs
         which we have elaborately formulated through history.
      Certainly the historical and literary representation
         of God's revelation of God's self to humankind has
         displayed [a] to broader view of God than possible
         within our own limited experience.
      Yet cognitive understanding of God is <u>not</u> sufficient;
         God is <u>known</u> and <u>Understood</u> through <u>direct</u>
         <u>relationship</u> in the presence of the Holy Spirit,
         scriptures, Jesus Christ on Earth, and through the
         lives and messages of others in the community of faith.
Learning: We (I/2 and S/2) must risk.
      The truth can, may be often offensive to people.
      Yet the risk and truth of relationship must be
         entered into and shared.
Evaluation: Pursue some of the questions that airse.

Feedback

The supervision goal for the month was to seek to make the
      sessions more "intimate."
Your goal statement is right on target. And your activity statement
     tells clearly how you intend to do it.

Your "report" is very textured this time.
Thanks.
It would help, I think, if you would connect it a bit more with
     the "activity" you state.
How did you "change the structure of the session?"
Obviously you are being energized by the last couple supervision
     sessions.
Is there something about the format that has helped?

You have made a good argument.
         To understand God requires us to be in relationship with God.
What that means is (I think you say) that we must be in direct
     relationship with one another in the presence of the Holy
     Spirit.
Now, how does that get done in your ministry at the Center?
I hope that you got to that question as you talked your argument
     through.
The theological language needs to be attached to real behavior.
Perhaps you can illustrate such a connection in a future log.
We need to know how those are made, since they are a core matter
     in supervision.

Yes, truth can be offensive.
So risk is part of ministry.
Again, this powerful point would have had more "bite" if your
     report had contained an illustration from your ministry
     where "truth" offended and how you experience/responded
     to that.
(This could also have occupied a log on "ministry assignment.")

LOG 3: Supervisor Two

Goal: Theology of the street
Activity: Continue dialogue on "why bother to save the church?"
Report: In this session we renewed our conversation around the
        future of the church.
    My basic "position" was/is that the church will die because
        of an inability to adequately reflect the spiritual
        experience of individuals it seeks to address.
    I/2 stated that she felt that, as in Romas 11, new people of
        God will be raised up to give witness to the world.
    The rise of liberation and Third world theologies could be a
        case in point.
    Through the discussion it became clear that I/2 and my
        definitions of the "church" were different.
    She defines it in the more classical sense of wherever 2 or
        more are gathered.
    I focus on a rejection of the PC(USA) for its pseudo-aware
        rhetoric and the various denominations (e.g., Baptist)
        that maintain a male dominated structure, etc.
Learning: When developing personal theologies and perspectives on
        the church, one must separate out the man-made
        structure from the God-ordained structure.
    I need to pursue the development of a critique that does
        this to a better degree.
Evaluation: Pursue difference in future sessions.

Feedback:
I take it that the question, "why bother to save the church?" is
        pretty much a rhetorical question for you.
If you defined it as I/2 does, you wouldn't need to bother -- God
        would do it for you.
If you define it as a human structure, then it must stand up under

        social scrutiny and will survive insofar as it does an important
        job.
"Bother" is not at issue.
Have I got it right?

If so, I think I'm in your court.
And I agree with you that "one must separate out the man-made
        [sic] structure from the god-ordained structure."
At least if you're going to dialogue with folk who believe in
        God's activity in the world.
Much of modern theology has struggled with just this matter.
Once the tripartite universe was disconfirmed, it was no longer
        possible to leave "God in heaven" and "humanity on earth."
The notion of relationship with others and worlds beyond ourself
        was introduced.
"Incarnation" came to be a complex of revelation and experience
        of selves beyond themselves.

So why do you or Rachel or anyone act in non-self-interest ways?
        But that is what you introduce in your next log.

APPENDIX 6

Coding of Log and Feedback Examples

    These are codings from the logs and feedback letters
presented in Appendix 5. The Sentence # listing refer as
follows: R = Log Report Sentence; L = Log Learning Sentence. The
sentence number within the log or feedback is given. Some
feedback letters started out with comments which were not
directly related to the log content. Those comments, while
playing an important role in initiating and sustaining the social
interaction of the logging-feedback process, have not been
included in the cataloging here.

LOG 3: Intern One (I/1)

Sentence #	Speech Act	Topic
R:1	Describing	Clash of values
R:2	Elaborating	Contrasting ideas of sharing
R:3	Describing	S/1's response
L:1	Asserting	Conflict is painful
L:2	Asserting	Youth need structure

Feedback

	Speech Act	Topic
1	Asserting	Good follow up prior log
2	Asserting	Sharing history is good idea
3	Describing	Psychologist's using "I"
4	Elaborating	What one ought to say

*****New Paragraph*****

	Speech Act	Topic
5	Asserting	Confusion over learning
6	Asserting/ Directing	Absence of loyalty Say more in interview
7	Elaborating	More info would help in understanding S/1's response

* * * * *

LOG 3: Supervisor One (S/1)

Sentence #	Speech Act	Topic
R:1	Describing	I/1's report on outing
R:2	Describing	I/1's particular response to kids
R:3	Describing	S/1's noting what was intolerable
R:4	Describing	Pressed I/1 for root of conflict
R:5	Describing	I/1's response clarified
R:6	Describing	Identified strategy
L:1	Asserting	Listening for conflict is key
L:2	Elaborating	If unnoticed, true conflict is passed

Feedback

	Speech Act	Topic
1	Asserting	Listening is important
2	Describing	From S/1, gap in I/1's log understood
3	Describing	FW describes his feedback to I/1
4	Asserting	Glad for S/1's persistence
5	Elaborating	Important for I/1 and S/1 to understand each other
6	Asserting	Importance of S/1's last sentence
7	Describing	I/1's position in logs
8	Elaborating	I/1 explains
9	Describing	S/1's indication of I/1's doubts
10	Asserting Belief	Doubt factored into ministry equals growth
11	Asserting	Such issues require response in supervision

* * * * *

LOG 3: I/2

Sentence #	Speech Act	Topic
R:1	Describing	Supervision activity
R:2	Describing	Nature of discussion
R:3	Asserting	Understanding of God
R:4	Describing	Key issue for both I/2 & S/2
R:5	Asserting	God as being
R:6	Elaborating	Being in relationship
		God's nature known in intimate relations
		Theological concepts have come through history
R:7	Asserting	God's revelation known through history and greater than personal knowledge
R:8	Asserting	Cognitive understanding of God is insufficient
R:9	Asserting	God known through HS, JC and through the faith community
L:1	Asserting	Personal risk is necessary
L:2	Assertion	Truth may be offensive
L:3	Elaborating	Risk and truth are prerequisite to relations

Feedback

1	Describing	Supervision goal for month
2	Describing	Statement goal is correct
3	Describing	Activity statement is accurate

*****New Paragraph*****

4	Describing	Textured report
5	Thanking	
6	Asserting	"It would be helpful to connect more
	Directing	with activity
7	Questioning	How was the session changed
8	Describing	Energy in last sessions seen
9	Questioning	Change in format helpful?

*****New Paragraph*****

10	Asserting	Good argument
11	Asserting	Relationship required to understand God
12	Conjecting	Relationship is presence of another with the HS
13	Questioning	How is that done at Center
14	Asserting	Hope that come up in supervision
15	Elaborating	Theo language must have real behavior
16	Directing	Relationship can be described in future log
17	Elaborating	Need to know how those connections are made

18	Asserting/Agreeing	Truth can be offensive
19	Asserting	Risk is part of ministry
20	Asserting/ Instructing	Powerful point could have been stronger if offensiveness could have been evidenced in report
21	Suggesting/ Directing	Could have been a ministry log

* * * * *

LOG 3:   S/2

Sentence #	Speech Acts	Topic
R:1	Describing	Conversation on church
R:2	Asserting	Church will die
R:3	Describing	I/2's belief
R:4	Describing/ Asserting	Liberation theol is a good case
R:5	Describing	Differences in "church" surface
R:6	Elaborating	I/2's view = where 2 or more gather
R:7	Elaborating	S/2's view = institutional
R:8	Describing	Rejection of Presbyterian and Baptist views
L:1	Asserting	Necessary to sort out human and God ordained structures
L:2	Asserting	S/2 needs more work on this
Feedback		
1	Interpreting	Why bother is rhetorical
2	Elaborating	For I/2 God works it out
3	Elaborating	Human structure holds up to do job
4	Restating	"Bother" is not issue
5	Questioning	Right?
6	Asserting	Discussion in your court
7	Asserting	FW agrees with distinctions
8	Elaborating	Necessary for dialogue
9	Elaborating	Modern theo's dilemma
10	Elaborating	Tripartite universe required new definitions
11	Elaborating	Worlds beyond self
12	Asserting	Incarnation became a complex
13	Questioning	Why not act in self-interest
14	Describing	This leads to next log

65

Response by Jack L. Seymour, Professor of Education
Garrett-Evangelical Theological Seminary

THEOLOGICAL LANGUAGE AND PROFESSIONAL EDUCATION: AN HISTORIAN'S RESPONSE

The methodologies of hermeneutics have been refined with written texts. While these methods have been helpful in practical theology and religious studies, an issue remains about whether approaches to interpret texts are also appropriate to the interpretation of "action" situations. David Steward and Rebecca Slough provide an intriguing exploration of potential methods to study an action situation of supervision as an alternate mode of theological education. They demonstrate how supervision and consultation are themselves acts of textual interpretation, some of which are written and others of which are expressed in living persons and situations.

Paul Ricoeur has argued that meaningful action could be treated as a text. For him, the methodologies of hermeneutics were appropriate to the study of dynamic situations, in particular, social science ("The Model of Text: Meaningful Action Considered As Text," Social Research 38 (Autumn 1971):529-562). His argument has been important for theological education, particularly in the expansion of field education. In this discussion, two issues have recurred: (1) assessing how the methodologies of interpretation are useful as tools for the practice of ministry and (2) determining how hermeneutics helps to frame a theology/theory of the practice of ministry.

First, recent texts in practical theology have sought to use hermeneutics to develop a method for ministry. An example is by Charles Winquist, Practical Hermeneutics: A Revised Agenda For Ministry (Chico, CA: Scholars Press, 1980). Winquist has argued that the method of ministry is "practical" hermeneutics. His approach illustrates how to "over-hear" the meanings present in the experiences of individuals to provide a wider horizon of meaning that integrates theological traditions with dynamic experience. Another illustration of the use of hermeneutic methodologies is the work of the pastoral theologian Charles Gerkin who builds on the theories of Ricoeur. See Widening the Horizons: Pastoral Responses to a Fragmented Society (Philadelphia: Westminster Press, 1986).

Second, others have used hermeneutics to reflect on the nature and recovery of practical theology. An example is the collection of essays Formation and Reflection: The Promise of Practical Theology (Philadelphia: Fortress Press, 1987), edited by Lewis Mudge and James Poling. This collection seeks to answer the question, "What is the relation between 'theology' as an academic discipline and living, worshipping, serving communities of faith?" (p. xiii).

Both of these conversations have stimulated serious questions about the effectiveness of the present "academy paradigm" for theological education embodied in the seminary. Steward and Slough review this literature well on pages 7 and 8. Therefore, their study on Teaching and Learning Practice is particularly important for the discussion of the emerging shape of theological education and for the exploration of hermeneutical methodologies for use in action situations. Their primary contribution is the exploration of four methods to assist student and teacher to interpret "meaningful action as text." Although they discovered the methods were uneven, they are to be applauded for convincing us that the search needs further sustained attention.

Rather than analyzing the benefits of each method as a relational hermeneutic, I will examine the assumptions which have shaped their project. Having been asked to work as a "revisionist" historian, I will suggest historical analysis as an additional method for their study and will consider their project as an historical text.

History is itself an activity of exploring and interpreting texts, only some of which are written. Revisionist history, in particular, is the clarification of the "ideological" frames of reference which "cause" us to interpret "events" in particular ways. Historians seek both to honor "events" recorded in texts and to draw inferences for understanding contemporary behavior. Every text, including the historical study itself, is written from a particular perspective. A "perspective" has caused many historical accounts to be guilty of presentism, that is, overlaying experiences from the present onto the past, or of creating a mythic past to fuel a contemporary ideology. Recognizing that fuel a contemporary ideology. Recognizing that perspective inevitably influences both the research and writing of a study, the historian uses a set of "rules" to clarify that influence. These rules include the following:

(1) the perspective of the author is made explicit,
(2) present issues motivating the study are clearly stated and examined,
(3) alternative sources of information are emphasized; contradictions in sources are highlighted,
(4) attention is given to clarifying alternatives to dominant patterns of social organization and to minority interpretations of experience, and
(5) conclusions are examined in relation to present opportunities for policy-making.

A key to revisionist history is making as explicit as possible the assumptions which motivate, inform, and control a study. (For a fuller development of these rules, see my article "Power and History: History as 'Critical' Analysis," Religious Education 82 Summer 1987 349-359).

ASSUMPTIONS

To analyze "Teaching and Learning Practice" as an historical project requires first the clarification of the perspective and assumptions which I bring to this study.

(1) Something is wrong with the teaching of the practice of ministry. Steward and Slough are correct about that. Research does not focus enough on the dynamics of the action situations - the practice of ministry. Instead, most teaching involves the learning of a vocabulary (jargon) which sets the "minister" (the professional) apart rather than that of concept formation for reflection on concrete experience. The "Introduction" and "Project" sections of this study represent an important critique of theological education.

(2) Nevertheless, the importance of learning theological jargon should not be under-emphasized. If language, to quote Vgotsky, focuses "... one's attention, selecting dis-tinctive features and analyzing and synthesizing them" (p. 5) and thereby defines what one sees, even "professional" language uncovers reality and focuses vision. The problem with professional languages is that they separate professionals from "clients." In theology, however, we must work to see that this is not the case, for theological language is to be a common language of the community of faith opening up horizons of meaning in the experience of people.

(3) An important alternative model for professional education is suggested in the work of Argyris and Schoen. Argyris demonstrates how "practice" is more adequately conceived as an experiment in action science. Schoen suggests an approach to the reformation of professional education through the use of supervisors/artists who are practitioners and scholars/teachers who are consultants. Practice itself can be treated as an experiment in education.

However, the use of supervisors in theological education has not been particularly successful. Field education supervisors have tended to function either "psychologically" or as masters apprenticing novices into traditional practice. In turn, most theological educators have not been trained to function as consultants.

More importantly, the very definition of the word "professional" has resulted in a "clerical" paradigm for ministry which itself is being seriously questioned by theologies of ministry of the marginalized. Many of the assumptions of "professionalism" conflict with emerging notions of theology. Therefore, we must be suspicious about the use of "professional" models of education. These may themselves be captured by ideologies in conflict with emerging notions of ministry. In particular, a study focused on education with the marginalized must seek to clarify the relationship of concepts such as "professional" and "people of God."

(4) The search for a definition of practice is crucial for the reformulation of theological education. The old theory/practice distinction is facile. Practice is much greater than skills or content. Steward and Slough are to be applauded for attempting inductively to define practice.

(5) Practically speaking, any research project conducted by a team on their innovation strategy at the same time that they are conducting the innovation becomes part

of it. All of the research efforts were therefore interventions of the consultant and activities in the innovation strategy.

THE METHOD OF HISTORICAL ANALYSIS

The task of the research project was stated as "Whether and how these structures (urban site, on-field classes, on-site supervision, spiritual direction, and academic consultation) work to train persons to minister is what we are exploring." Therefore, determining whether the Network Center for the Study of Christian Ministry was an effective model of theological education integrating "church" and seminary was the focus of the study and grant. This broader goal was further refined in the abstract as "Supervision and consultation are identified as the two teaching/learning relationships on which the study will focus."

Normally strategies to evaluate a project like this would be empirical and follow the methods of policy evaluation. The authors' method however was "inductive," using an analysis of logs to explore the felt-experience (the meanings made) of the primary participants. This method provided significant information on the dynamics of two relationships in NCSCM, the supervisory and consultative ones. It however did not address the other "structures" in the teaching/learning design. They sought to speak to the larger issue of effectiveness of the project through inference from participant reports.

How could historical methods be used in assessing the project? Could we determine in the midst of the project or can we determine now the effectiveness of NCSCM and its design? Below are four suggestions for possible directions.

(1) Most simply, the logs are historical texts, like diaries. They reveal a person's particular perceptions of events and what they define as important. Moreover, since the logs are written for public consumption, even if only to the consultants, what is written in the logs is guarded by the knowledge that it will reflect on the author. All of the techniques appropriate to question the "accuracy" and meaning of the content of diaries is appropriate to this study.

(2) More importantly, history provides a means of exploring the trajectory of the innovation. An historical analysis could help to determine the "choice point" when the decision to organize the NCSCM was made. At this time, there were reasons for the founding of the center. It could have been a felt-need, the desire for innovation, or a variety of other reasons. This decision sorted through options, some of which were probably unspoken, in choosing a particular pattern. The decision then created a rationale that became an assumptive framework for the project. Many elements of this framework were stated; others probably were not. The framework, however, provided a perspective for the designers as they recruited participants and conducted research. Also the framework naturally caused them to attend to particular data and to ignore other data. This focusing of vision is particularly true with an inductive design as Steward and Slough chose. In other words, a testing, a careful analysis, of the "ideology" which motivated the innovation and research is crucial to judging the findings. Some limited attention is given to this issue on pages 6-8. An historical analysis would expand it.

(3) Moreover, each of the agencies that agreed to participate in the project, as well as each of the participants, had a framework for their decisions. The two centers are in the business of ministry. For them, the training is secondary. This fact is apparent in actions at the second site. Training is thus an intrusion, even if desired, into an action situation. The ideology and agenda of the sites powerfully shape the content and structure of education at those sites. In the study, we do not enter enough into these motivating factors for students, supervisors, and sites. As a result, we do not know how to evaluate what they report and attend to in their log reports and why particular themes are important or ignored. For example, why did the supervisor in site 1 function as a "clinical" supervisor and how did the fact that the student desired such "pastoral" supervision influence the outcomes of education?

(4) All innovations take place in a dynamic context. Supervision and consultation were not the only two factors influencing the theological learnings of the students and of the researchers. History can assist us in drawing the ecology of influences in an educational environment. To evaluate the effectiveness of the center as an alternative form of theological education, it is imperative that we describe as clearly as possible

the ecology for the educational strategies within the project and as broadly as possible the interface of this project with the wider educational ecology of the students. Such a question assists us in knowing which relationships to explore for their significance in the causality of learning. I have discovered in evaluations of field education that the site is more powerful than the supervision and that the reflection in the academy is more transformatory than supervisory reflection on-site. Methodologically, the educational history of Lawrence Cremin is particularly useful in drawing the larger ecology for learning. In <u>American Education: The National Experience, 1783-1876</u> (New York: Harper & Row, 1980), Cremin describes the ecological interaction of educational structures and demonstrates how a particular biography is "formed" within these structures.

History cannot by itself determine the effectivness of an innovation like NCSCM. However, it can contribute to the policy climate in which decisions are to be made. History can clarify influences in the context, reveal the intentionalities of participants, and define reasons that alternatives were ignored at the choice point when the decision for the project was made. As an hermeneutical effort, history expands our awareness of the "personal interests" that affect both the learning and the conclusions.

ASSUMPTIONS ABOUT PRACTICE

"Teaching and Learning Practice" is a fine exploration of action science. The paper fits the assessment of Argyris on p. 37, "less precision does not preclude the lack of rigor." It is a thorough attempt to discern action in a supervisory relationship. Nevertheless, the study leaves the reader feeling that something is missing.

If the paper had been defined as a critical exploration of four hermeneutical methods for analyzing a relationship in professional education, the reader would have been satisfied. While desiring further comparison of the methods, the reader would have explored the implications of the principles for supervision and consultation listed on pp.34-42. In particular, the description about concept formation and theological language in the section on Consultation Principles is satisfying. It provides the rationale for rethinking theological education. The description relates to a notion being discussed by theologians about redefining theology as "reflective praxis." See Peter Hodgson, <u>Revisioning the Church: Ecclesial Freedom in the New Paradigm</u>, (Philadelphia: Fortress Press, 1988), p. 19.

However, the paper promises the reader more than a methodological exploration into the supervisory relationship. The reader expects an examination of the effectiveness of the center as an alternative site for theological education. In addition, the reader expects a discussion of the practice and effectiveness of youth ministry conducted at each site and a discussion of the skills in practice gained by the participants in the project. (See the goal statements on page 5, the description of the models of youth ministry, and the assumptions about youth articulated on pages 5 and 6.

Moreover, compared to the rigor of the analysis of the logs, the conclusions about professional schooling at the end of Part III are impressionistic. For example, we are not clear about what specific practice the students learned in the field sites and what learnings resulted from the other components of the teaching design. In fact, the data suggests that student 2 learned more about "avoiding" youth ministry by focusing on the other professional staff, i.e., professional peers. Even though the first conclusion on pages 43-44 makes conceptual sense, it is not demonstrated. A definition of practice is not presented nor is a concrete exploration of the practice of youth ministry at each site.

In addition, the second conclusion (page 44) seems to conflict with the data presented about supervision. In these two cases, on-site supervision did not transform the practice of the student. Supervisor 1 and Intern 1 came to a closer mutual understanding of their view of ministry. This result is to be expected by the close personal nature of their clinical model of supervision. However, it is not clear that their mutual notion is effective practice on the site nor does it provide the kind of ministerial transformation powerfully advocated by the authors in their assumptions on page 7. On the other hand, neither Supervisor 2 nor Intern 2 "... expanded his/her own thinking structure (and thus did not expand her/his action patterns) with regard to ministry" (page 27). Supervision did not seem to be the basic effective teaching/learning relationship.

The effective relationship seems to have been that of consultation. The last conclusion about the importance of the faculty scholar/teacher in consultation is clearly warranted by the data. In fact, the consultant's intervention and the research project were the key effective ingredients in this project.

Why this lack of reader satisfaction and why this conflict of conclusions about professional schooling? An historical analysis of the project and the research could help to answer these questions. While I do not have enough data to demonstrate adequately the following conclusions, I suggest that the sample the authors had to work with was so small and the methods so difficult that they became fascinated by the exploration of the methods for studying practice, rather than with the practice itself. Moreover, the bold strokes of the conclusions on pages 43-45 replicate the conclusions about professional educa-tion defined by Schoen in Educating the Reflective Practitioner (San Francisco: Jossey Bass, 1987), a source on which they rely.

Historical analysis needed to be an important part of this study. An exploration of the founding and assumptions of the NCSCM and an examination of the assumptions of the researchers were needed. The history and assumptions of each of the sites was also essential information to understand how education occurred within them. Moreover, attention needed to be given to defining the ecological relationship of the educational components of the study and the context for learning within which the study was conducted. As the authors conclude, "... language must function in situ - where professional practice happens. The practitioner works by figuring things out. Concepts make this possible. Language is the tool to facilitate the process. Learning practice is, importantly, learning to use language to figure things out" (p. 45). This states an important research agenda. What language did the students learn, was it effective, and where did they learn it? Further reflection on these questions requires additional historical and ideological analysis. I hope this paper stimulates just such reflection.

CONCLUSION

Steward and Slough are to be commended for the importance of their project for theological education. They encourage us to explore further a series of important questions.

(1) We need to define "practice." In common usage, the word is defined too broadly. How can we improve the teaching of practice if it seems to mean everything that a professional (practitioner) does? In particular, how do we define reflective practice (praxis) and transform practice to be genuinely mutual and just (as the theology of ministry articulated by the authors suggests)?

(2) We need further hermeneutical skills to read and clarify the texts of supervision. In particular, we need to ask how the reflection on "practical hermeneutics" or practical theology provides research methods from within the discipline of theology to study these interventions of religious language. We may find that theological education is itself for both church member and professional a "community understood language" designating experiences of response to the Holy (page 66).

(3) We need further reflection on the relation of seminary to ministerial education and on the role of the teacher/scholar. "Faculty need to become language teachers" (p. 45). If all thought is analogical (p. 43), then theological reflection by both people and priest is also analogical. (See Gordon Kaufman's discussion of theological language in Theology for a Nuclear Age, Philadelphia: Westminster Press, 1985.) Language determines the meaning given to experience and the interventions allowed to be thought. The consultant provided a depth to the work of the NCSCM project through his "conceptual play." We need to continue to explore theological education as an exercise in imaginative play - a reflective praxis on ecclesial experience. Education may provide the "professional" with an imaginative frame with which to organize and focus experience and a set of metaphors by which to choose interventions that continue the play about those experiences we name justice, transformation, and wholeness.

Response by Margaret S. Steward, Professor of Clinical Psychology
         University of California Davis Medical Center, Sacramento

How is professional practice taught and learned? This question was asked by a theologian, committed to assist students develop competence in the practice of ministry, and interested also in determining the parameters of the teaching and learning of practice which hold across the professional disciplines. This paper reports the results of a pilot study targeted on supervisors and interns in an alternative setting for education of urban ministry. In order to study the process of the mastery of practice, David Steward chose to link himself dyadically in a consultative relationship with two supervisors and with two interns, and to open that data to analysis. Thus rather than the more conventional direct observation and analysis of the interactions between a supervisor and an intern, each participant spoke for him/herself. Utilizing a variety of formats provided by the research director and his team, each supervisor and intern selected the content to report out of the constant flow of their professional interactions with others.

This study was conceived within the framework of action science (C. Argyris, R. Putnam, and D. Smith, Action Science. San Francisco: Jossey-Bass Publishers, 1985). At least one strategy for the evaluation of the action science focus can be found in the multimethod approach advocated three decades ago by D. T. Campbell and D. W. Fiske (1959, "Convergent and Discriminant Validation by the Multitrait-Multimethod Matrix" Psychological Bulletin 56: 81-105), and that remains the meta-strategy of choice today when studying interpersonal processes. M. S. Clark and H. T. Reis (1988), authors of the most recent review of the research on interpersonal processes ("Interpersonal Processes in Close Relationships" Annual Review of Psychology 39:609-72) find that laboratory experiments with strangers and survey of individuals predominate the field. Neither is satisfactory to understand the complexity of interpersonal process - especially if the focus is modification and growth of the individuals and the relationship over time.

In this project case study, self-report, interview, and standardized personality tests are utilized for data collection. No data are more compelling to a listener/reader than those reported by the case study method - although none offer a more difficult assignment to separate the "species-specific" phenomena from the generalizable. Self-report data, seen particularly in the self-selection of episodes to log, provide some needed protective features in what might otherwise be experienced as an invasion into the territory of clinical supervision. The analysis of the clinically generated material through metaphorical analysis, and speech act theory reflect differing states of the art and science across the disciplines at this point in time. The simplist, though psychometrically the most sophisticated, analysis is of changes in role perception. Taken together this offers the reader a "thickly textured" set of original material, and diverse analyses.

Because the experience of all participants is sampled several times over the course of the year-long project, the data collected during this project provide a window into the supervisory relationship between supervisor and intern as it evolved throughout the year. Simultaneously and interactively, the contracted consultative relationship between the scholar/researcher and both supervisor and intern evolved as well. The nature of these dyadic relationships is such that often the content of each set of interactions consisted of reflections on their relationships with others. Thus the research process focused on individuals who as a direct result of their supervisory relationship and their consultative relationship were able to focus reflectively on interpersonal relationships with others. The subjects are simultaneously "in" on the research at the same time as they are sometimes distracted by it, while struggling with the people in their real life clinical/pastoral work settings. This is the core content of mastery of the practice of ministry.

What are the contributions of this research to our understanding of the mastery of the practice of ministry? I believe there are several

(1) to the growing literature on interpersonal processes. This is a literature which has been limited by focus on strangers or lovers (Huston, H. L., and Levinger, G. (1978) "Interpersonal Attraction and Relationships" Annual Review of Psychology 29: 115-56; Clark, M. S. and Reis, H. T. (1988) "Interpersonal Processes in Close Relationships" in M. R. Rosenzweig and L. W. Porter, ed., Annual Review of Psychology 39:609-72) and has

ignored until very recently the other constellations of persons in relationship - such as in this study, where direct data come from relationships between the researcher/consultant supervisors and interns, and indirect data is available about the supervisor-intern relationships, and intern-congregation relationship.

(2) to the literature on development of relationships over time. Sequential logs written by both supervisors and interns give the flavor, and codable changes in the movement toward changes in role perception and role behavior - both offer perspectives on competent practice within the ever enfolding awareness of the realities of the context.

What are the limitations of this pilot study? Again there are several that come to mind.

(1) The sample of supervisors (two males), interns (one male, one female) and consultant (one male) dramatically limit the generalizability of the findings. The process needs to be replicated to determine the features unique to the chemistry of the particular supervisor-intern dyad, and to the disciplinary focus of the faculty member, and to determine those features which hold across. D. A. Kenny ("What makes a Relationship Special?" in T. Draper, ed. Methods to Study Families Beverly Hills: Sage, 1987) has suggested in his Social Relations Model the necessity to cross subjects so that they interact with multiple partners. Thus one might separate the tendency of the actors to elicit/display a behavior only to a specific partner, from the tendency for each to display or elicit such behavior independent of those to whom they are related.

(2) There was no direct sampling of the supervisor-intern interaction. Limitations of time, and money could be mentioned. However, this omission may well have been critically supportive of the development of a supervisory relationship precisely because it was "unmonitored." By virtue of the privacy given the supervisory relationship, similar to the function of the bedroom door, both the supervisor and the intern may have been more willing to handle the scrutiny of on-going consultative relationship with the researcher.

Were the right dimensions selected for study? In order to answer that question I began to muse, and then to systematically reflect on the two most extreme experiences which I have had in the mastery of practice - the first as a teacher, the second as a learner.

I am a child clinical psychologist and a professor at U. C., Davis, School of Medicine. In medical education today there is probably more demand on the student for action and less time for reflection than in any other professional school. The pacing is often frantic, and there is time to get everything done only if sleep is considered a luxury, not a necessity. In this world the "see one, do one, teach one" rubric seems to hasten everything along.

Nearly everything which a medical student does is mediated verbally. Symptoms are initially verbally described by patients. Medical students recite these to one another, and rehearse patient symptoms and resulting strategies in daily rounds with residents and faculty. They document in writing every step of the process. In a teaching hospital, a patient's medical record might contain four written versions of each examination, procedure, decision; written by a third year medical student, a first year resident, the chief resident, and a faculty supervisor.

I am also a moccasin maker. This is a title bestowed on me by my Tlingit Indian teacher, Esther Littlefield, in May 1975, following a year-long tutorial with her, during a sabbatical in Alaska. As I reflect back on it, I see it now as a fascinating year. I remember it also as humbling, frustrating, and ultimately growth producing. The experience challenged my understanding of what it meant to be a teacher, a learner, a master practitioner. It expanded my experience of myself beyond the role of an impatient, somewhat arrogant "fast study" to an awareness of my potential as a slow learner. I am grateful for the willingness of my teacher to offer and sustain a supervisory relationship within which I mastered both an ancient art and a bit of myself.

Words provided a context for my learning, but unlike my experience in the "lower 48," words were not used for instruction, or correction, or reinforcement. Through words the old stories were told. My teacher told of her childhood, and of her mother's childhood. I did not first weave a basket to hold my leather scraps, nor did I tan the leather, but through the stories I came to understand where those steps would have come in the process in an earlier time. Over the year I also learned that my teacher spoke, I did not. When I hit a problem, I learned not to ask questions. I had to wait for her to come upon the same problem and then observed how she solved it. When I thought I understood how to tie a particular bead knot, I was not to talk with enthusiasm or bravado about it, but rather simply to use it. Neither could I talk my way out of a mistake - with an apology of good intentions gone awry, nor with a promise of doing it better with another piece of leather "next time."

Not only was the end product important, the process was critical. I had to take out a whole section of beadwork because I had done it too quickly and was not sufficiently respectful of the beads, the thread, the needle or the old woman who first saw the design in the snow. For the same reason somewhat later, I had to rip out and repleat the leather toe of one moccasin three times, work that required great precision and physical strength. My hands were bleeding when I finally finished the third effort. Mid-year a visiting colleague of mine asked my teacher if it was difficult to teach a white woman. Although I thought we were getting along rather well, and that I was becoming a model student, my teacher noted two big problems: I still talked too much, and I "hurry-hurried."

The world of the moccasin maker and the medical student provide striking polar opposites along a number of dimensions - neither, of course, totally encompasses the world of ministry through each overlap sufficiently to suggest further exploration of some variables. In the framing of action science, the query is what problems have been set by this research that might be addressed next?

(1) some fine tuning of the pacing of the broad range tasks/expectations and experiences which are involved in ministry. Some are best dealt with slowly, others need to be handled at a faster pace. In "the next study," use might be made of the personal diary. For example, every social interaction which lasts longer than 10 minutes might be noted, and provide grist for the supervisory mill, and a fine data source for the researcher.

(2) a more subtle treatment of the role of language/action in the development and mastery of professional practice. Who speaks, who listens? What is the context for language/action? Do the words provide a framework for action, command action, elicit or compel action, and/or invite reflection? The seminal work of Vygotsky might well provide the context for this kind of analysis (J. V. Wertsch, 1985, Culture, Communication and Cognition: Vygotskian Perspectives. New York: Cambridge University Press).

(3) a study of the impact of the supervisor-intern relationship after it has been artificially terminated by the realities of the supervision contract which end with the school year. While there is considerable theory and research on the initial impressions of a dyadic relationship, and some work on the development of relationships, there is essentially no work on the "post-mortem" period. Many of us who have worn both hats - as classroom teachers and clinical supervisors - believe that the professioanl life far more profoundly than academic course work. Some of us have heard our own words come back as wisdom - or banality - from the mouths of our own eminent, former students.

(4) a study of the most effective timing of the intervention by a consulting faculty member not just to monitor, but to evaluate for supervisor/intern match. Research suggests that with a sharp increase in giving of goods, services and support in the first six weeks of a new relationship, there is likely to be the development of a close and satisfying relationship. While in the relationship that remains distant, there is a steady decline in benefits given from the early stages (J. H. Berg and M. S. Clark, "Differences in Social Exchange Between Intimate and Other Relationships: Gradually Evolving or Quickly Apparent?" in Friendship and Social Interaction, V. J. Derlaga and B. A. Winstead, ed. New York: Springer Verlag, 1986; 101-28). Even without sampling directly the supervisor/intern interaction, the logs might give a clue to the quality of the developing relationship, so that good matches might be supported, and participants in stagnant or deteriorating matches might be reassigned.

Response by Sara Little, Critz Professor of Christian Education
        Union Theological Seminary, Virginia,

        Out of a broad interest in theological education in general, and the teaching and
learning of practice in particular, this respondent will approach the task with comments
on the contribution of this research to these interests, and then formulate some questions
that could be raised as next steps for investigation. This interest is reflected in the
respondent's relationship to the Youth Ministry and Theological Schools Project noted in
the report, administrator for Union Theological Seminary in Virginia for the Lilly funded
grant which helped support the project under consideration. References to methodology,
both theoretical sources and procedural evaluation, are intentionally bypassed in favor of
attention to the two areas indicated, with the hope that other respondents will be
available for methodological analysis.

        With respect to theological education in general, which includes but is not limited
to theological schooling, the report of research under consideration makes a significant
contribution to the understanding of the relationship of theory and practice. That is to
say, concerns about youth, about ministry, and about schooling are examined and tested in
the context of practice. Potentially, revision of the assumptions could occur, and the
resulting projection of action units and reflective procedures changed accordingly. Those
assumptions seem to be more confirmed than questioned. In any case, what we have held out
to us is a procedure which could be self-consciously held up as a way to engage in a
continuing reflection on theological education in general.

        H. Richard Niebuhr, reporting on a major study of theological education in this
century, in The Purpose of the Church and Its Ministry (1956), called for just such an
approach. He said that one cannot understand the functioning of ministry without engaging
in its practice. Yet learning by doing is not the answer. Reflection, which "precedes,
accompanies, and follows action" is essential, not only for learning the meaning of deeds,
but also for relating those deeds to "a whole world beyond." Niebuhr was talking about the
nature of theory and the work of a theological school in an approach consistent with the
research reported. That approach could in fact be viewed as a framework within which the
conclusions of this project could be consolidated and expanded. The project design
utilizes recent developments in social sciences and linguistic studies, which provides
sharper tools of analysis and refined formulations of learnings, and thus enables the
contributions to theoretical understanding of both ministry and the nature of schooling.
The researchers, like Niebuhr, reject the assumption that theory can be learned and then
applied, or that Bible and theology can give rise to foundational propositions from which
implications for practice can be deduced. (As a matter of fact, it would be interesting in
the content speech analysis to devise a scheme for testing whether any understandings
derived from detached schooling contexts did in fact become useful in the context of
practice. But this would be another project design.)

        Attention to the teaching and learning of practice, the focus of the research,
eventuated in some supervision principles which could serve as interpretive guides. Those
principles seem tailor-made for the kind of supervision that would be appropriate for
theological schooling. The principles of "match" and of "recursion" seem especially
promising for improving the quality of supervision that presently exists. What is
projected here is in many ways different from the concept of supervision set forth in
other areas of professional education, as teacher education, for example, or in business.
It deserves to be developed. Equally promising is the beginning articulation of the role
of the scholar/teacher, a role that up to this point has not been envisioned as it is
interpreted in the report.

        Consider a question about each of these areas of interest. How can reflection on
the practice of ministry contribute to the church's theological understanding, to its
formulation and reformulation of the tradition? Clearly beyond the scope of this
research, such a question naturally emerges from the report. The whole approach is
consistent with George Lindbeck's cultural-linguistic approach to religion, presented in
his The Nature of Doctrine (1984). Religions are seen as "comprehensive interpretive
schemes" which organize "all of life, including both behavior and belief." Lindbeck's
approach is not a one-way street from belief analyzed for implications for behavior.

Rather, there is a dialectic relation between religion and experience, where each realm interprets the other. The approach is much more comprehensive than is hinted at here, but the point should be clear - that what is formulated out of reflection in or on action can contribute not only to a theory of education for the teaching and learning of practice, but also to the content of theology for the church's "interpretive schemes." Similarly, perhaps even more directly, David Tracy's explication of a revisionist model of theology, in Blessed Rage for Order (1975), calls for a hermeneutical method where what is sought is a correlation between the two principal sources for theology, "Christian texts and common human experience and language." What emerges from a look at these two theologians is the thesis that the method set forth by David Steward could be expanded to make a contribution to theological education beyond the teaching and learning of practice. How can knowledge be interpreted, embodied, internalized, re-formulated? Although the focus of the research could have been diffused if expanded to engage in such questions, the broader framework of theological education could at some point be posed as a hermeneutical understanding consistent with the task investigated here.

The second question has to do with the supervisory and consultative plan for the teaching and learning of practice. How could the role of scholar/teacher in particular, as well as that of the supervisor, be construed so that they could balance and expand the intern's "interpretive scheme" for viewing the world? The relational context and the task focus were appropriate for the research design. Theological statements were obviously made, but neither the content analysis nor the description of the interventions gives a clear picture af the scope of processing that would be consistent with the wholistic concerns and goals advocated in the paper. Again, that would be a "next step," an expansion. It would be consistent with the theology of praxis advocated by numerous theologians, such as David Tracy. The scholar/teacher as consultant might well bring his/her scholarly discipline to bear on the discussions. The role of the second faculty person mentioned in the description of the project is not clear. Was there an opportunity to bring professional scholarly insights to bear on the learning?

The reason for raising this question is hard to state. The assumption is that ministry is to be understood and practiced not just out of a direct analysis of ministry, but also out of the broad-based theological commitments which serve as interpretive schemes to interact with culture and personal analysis. What happens is not only that ministry is enhanced, but also that the theological perspectives are tested, internalized, and become functional in ministry. In another of the Youth Ministry and Theological Schools projects, where the action unit was basic to the enterprise, one intern summarized an intense period of struggle with the statement, "Now I know the meaning of deliverance!" What he was enabled to do in the conversation was to draw on the previous year's study of Exodus to interpret present experience, thus moving to a new level of understandin@ of a concept. Such explorations as these grow out of an effort to achieve the underlying theological unity that seems to be fervently desired as an improvement over the fragmentation of theological education. It has to do with the integration of knowledge, which perhaps best occurs in the context of action. The self-understanding of the pastoral department of Union Theological Seminary in Virginia includes its intention to "bring the Christian tradition to bear on the tasks of ministry." Certainly such a possibility exists in the project, and in fact was enacted in a way that could be expanded.

In summary, the long-range possibilities of the contribution to theological education in general is increasingly apparent as one reflects on what happened. The development of conceptual structures which enhance theoretical and theological interpretation will be the desired next steps emerging from the project.

Response by Rev. David C. Duncombe, San Francisco

My approach to the study paper is that of a clinical pastoral education (CPE) supervisor who has used and valued the "action/reflection" model of clinical teaching for twenty rears with divinity students learning to minister to hospital patients, street people, and university students. The principal issue that the paper raises for me has to do with the structure and use of the reflection-eliciting mechanisms of supervision. The diagram below describes my understanding of this structure with respect to the modes of primary communication employed.

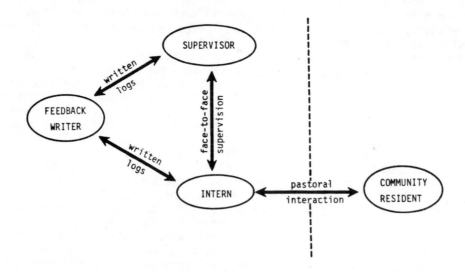

If this represents a fair picture of the flow and form of primary communication in the proposed model of supervision, a number of concerns are presented for me. The most striking perhaps is the asymmetry of the model. Most of the actors and transactions are on the left-hand side of what I would consider the focal action, the pastoral relationship between the intern and the community resident. Why do we build our models of supervision in such lopsided fashion? As a CPE supervisor, I can claim no better for my own models or practice. But it does seem curious that most of the reflection, "conversation," feedback loops, and participants rest on the shoulders of the intern, and it is the intern who seems to be the principal source of all information generated in the model about his or her pastoral relationships.

How is it that we make so little use of the information that might be given us by the person being ministered to? I am immediately aware of the logistical difficulties of eliciting, gathering, and classifying such information. But I think at the heart of our supervision models is an elitist assumption that the average patient, street person, or community resident has little to teach us about what is going on in a pastoral relationship - or perhaps can't express it in ways valuable to us. How many of those persons ministered to by I-1 and I-2 could have handled the categories required of logging, or even described in ways that we could understand the pastoral dynamics which they were experiencing.

When we add on a research component, it is even more difficult to escape the asymmetry of the model. We need intelligent, available, cooperative, motivated, and reliable respondents to complete an Adjective Check List or other psychometric tests. My elitist bias tells me that I won't find such qualities in the pool of community residents I minister to; so I turn to the side of the pastoral relationship where I can get such information. In doing so I am reminded of the old joke of the drunk standing under the lamp post at midnight looking for his keys. When someone asked him if he lost them there, he replies: "I don't think so, but at least there's some light here."

Are there alternative models? I had moderate success with one in an interprofessional course on chronic illness (see David C. Duncombe, "Five Years at Yale; 'The Seminar on the Chronically Ill,'" The Journal of Pastoral Care 27 (September 1974): 152-163). Each student followed a chronically ill patient who was regarded as his or her primary teacher. The "patient-teacher's" role was to help the student understand what it was like to be chronically ill. This understanding happened through the patient-teacher's developing relationship with the student - just by talking and visiting. At the end of the course, both the patient-teachers and the course supervisors evaluated the students. Why I have never carried this more symmetrical model into the teaching and supervising of pastoral relationships, I don't know. So I am left wondering what it would be like to build in some reflection and feedback loops on the right-hand side of the model with forms of communication more appropriate to the world of the counselee.

Let me turn next to the intern-supervisor relationship. The model suggests a teaching-by-example method not unlike those found in many parish internship programs. The assumption is that the intern learns by observing and interacting with the pastor supervisor. The S-1, I-1 pair seemed to work well together but the S-2, I-2 pair did not. The study is at its best when identifying and discussing the reasons why these pairs fared the way they did. We see that when intern and supervisor share approximately the same psychological needs, ideas of supervision, contexts of interpretation, and metaphors of ministry, supervision works better than when this is not the case. Yet I am left wondering whether the S-2, I-2 pair might have worked better had their differences been identified at the beginning of the relationship and the intern challenged to "try on" S-2's style - instead of being continually frustrated by it.

Alternatively, the supervisor can avoid a good bit of resistance by and confusion of the intern by helping the intern think through and work out of the intern's own doctrine of ministry - and not the supervisor's. I have used this latter method of supervision with divinity students ministering to street people (see David C. Duncombe, "Street-ministry CPE: An Experiment in the Haight-Ashbury," The Journal of Pastoral Care 42 September 1988). Where there are few external structures to provide pastoral identity, as on the streets, the experience of ministering out of one's own tradition and theology - facilitated and encouraged by the supervisor - can minimize the dissonance caused by supervisor-intern dissimilarities in basic values or style of ministry.

The model's logging component reminded me of the theatrical convention of spoken "asides": the two protagonists converse with one another, then, turning to the audience with a cupped hand, give their own (often different) interpretations of the just-completed interaction. The model's written logs serve as these asides, directed at the feedback writer and not at the other interaction participant. The feedback writer then responds in the same manner with a private communication privy only to the log writer.

In CPE, the supervisor and intern both write out their own impressions of an experience or of the supervisory relationship that they share. Presumably it serves the same purpose as log writing - that of promoting reflection. But then these impressions are read, not by a third party, but by the other half of the supervisory relationship. The ensuing discussion at the next supervisory session can explore directly the possibly differing perceptions of the same shared interaction or event. While I think the extended loop including the feedback writer adds an important dimension to the model, it should not be at the expense of the more direct reflective feedback possible between intern and supervisor.

One further addition to the model might be suggested: that of interactive supervision. When I am engaged in interactive supervision, I am working along side of my intern in a common task of ministry. This enables me to make direct observations of his or her behavior and immediate comments on it. Likewise, I encourage my intern to observe me in ministry, to question, criticize, and reflect. Since we are ministering together, we can reflect on the ways the other aids or inhibits our common goal. Where interactive supervision occurs, the supervisor need not rely solely on the intern's memory and perception of a ministry event. The result is a new feedback loop that adds more information to the system (see David C. Duncombe, "The Trivial Nature of CPE," Journal of Pastoral Care 42 March 1988).

Having tinkered around with a model that I basically admire and respect, reweighting it it here, adding or subtracting something there, let me close with two critical observations. The first has to do with its many uses. Not only is it a model for learning ministry, it is a model of supervision for the practice of ministry and a model for the study of both. That may be too much. Can one model handle learning, practice, and research? That would surely be an "elegant" model, but may be more cumbersome than efficient.

The other observation has to do with what I intuit as the basic goals and presuppositions of the study model itself. Unless I'm mistaken, the model points toward a non-dualistic pedagogy and method for reflecting on it, a pedagogy that would go beyond the common meaning of the word "relational" to something that envisions a "whole" apart from the individuals who interact within it. The model's concepts, constructs, metaphors, and analyses point toward this whole but are limited by the very thought and speech used to make it function. The most extreme example of this is the rampant individualism presupposed by the "needs" orientation of the Adjective Check List. Even needs for relationship presuppose a solipsistic world in which the other is object.

How we can move from a mindset which habitually starts with the "I" to one that is rooted in "we", let alone "the world", staggers the imagination. Noam Chomsky has done a great service in showing us how much our language binds us to the "I" paradigm, and excludes us from wholeness of being. Perhaps only mysticism has evolved a counter language, and at its most effective, its grammar is silence.

MINUTES OF THE COLLOQUY OF 13 MARCH 1988

List of Participants

Professors at the Graduate Theological Union

    David S. Steward (Religous Education)
    James Duke (Historical Theology)
    Thomas Leahy (New Testament)
    Wilhelm Wuellner (New Testament)

Professor at the University of California, Berkeley

    William S. Anderson (Classics)

Guests

    Margaret Steward (University of California, Davis)
    Sandra Luft (San Francisco State University)
    Thandeka (San Francisco State University)

Students

    Ed Bodanske
    Annette Moran
    Rebecca Slough
    Don Steele

MINUTES OF THE COLLOQUY OF 13 MARCH 1988

The Discussion

<u>D.Steward:</u>The written responses were very interesting to me. They present a wide variety of specific issues that I care about. Let me direct your attention, first, to the diagrams I brought, by way of a kind of overview of our intention in this project. As I surveyed the literature in professional theological schooling, I found that virtually all that literature dealt with courses that are to be offered and the disciplinary attachments of those courses. We want to look at professional schooling another way.

In my first diagram I state three things it seems to me that people who study professional schooling are able to work on. One has to do with the content of some tradition or knowledge base. This kind of information usually gets organized through introductory courses in a fairly transmissive fashion. In addition, professional schooling attempts to get some skills training done. Skills training is usually accomplished through some form of repetition - e.g., see one, do one, teach one.

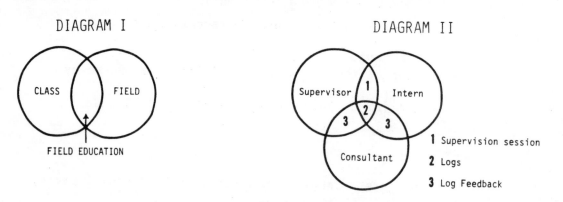

DIAGRAM I

CLASS   FIELD

FIELD EDUCATION

DIAGRAM II

Supervisor   1   Intern

2

3   2   3

Consultant

1 Supervision session

2 Logs

3 Log Feedback

We're attempting to study a third aspect of professional schooling, what I've called "practice." Practice is still an open concept for us. It has to do, we believe, with learning concepts - where concepts are active and where conceptualizing is something one does. The medical analog of practice might be diagnosis, where particular bits and pieces are somehow put together on the way to deciding about treatment. In the paper, I use the metaphor of play to get at how that work is done. And I use the code words throughout the paper of "concept generation," "concept formation," and "concept use," to get at what I think we're coming to call practice.

The second diagram deals with the structure of the teaching-learning interaction. Those of you who had the written responses will remember that David Duncombe took us to task for focusing on the abstract-intellectual side of things at the expense of the field-situational side. From his diagram I've taken what I call the traditional assumption that the arenas of class and field overlap, with field education occuring in the shared area in between. This is a setting-oriented way to think about schooling. You do different things in different places. What happens in classes, and what happens in the field, are different because of the class and field nature of the setting.

In this paper we're proposing a more interactional form. For the moment get rid of the site or the geographical context and look at the individuals who are involved in schooling. In our project the supervisor and the intern relate with one another in the supervision session by themselves. The logging procedure involves three parties: intern, supervisor and consultant. The log feedback involves the consultant with supervisor and the consultant with intern. The thing that's intriguing to us is that all persons who comes into this transaction bring a world with them. One does not need to eliminate from an interation analysis all the setting considerations that are part of the traditional diagram. But the second diagram can be adjusted to pick up more or less of an individual's world, or more or less extensive interaction. Each of the circles in the second diagram can be rotated in a variety of ways. I'd like to play with that in terms of an approach to schooling where practice is of concern. My intention is not to get rid of the geographical setting as an important element. It is to reconceptualize schooling so that setting does not frame the schooling; rather, the people in the interaction frame the schooling.

There are four different kinds of questions that I would be very interested to have us explore. The first set of questions have to do with the research perspective that we chose. We attempted to do "action research" as Chris Argyris has spelled it out. Action research involves the notion that research can be conducted as one intervenes in something. Our action perspective requires, we believe, a multidisciplinary approach. The approach of any given discipline will answer certain questions and will leave other questions unaddressed that need to be dealt with in an interactive topic, such as we propose. How would you critique our research perspective, and on what grounds?

A second area of questions has to do with the linguistic analysis of interaction. We could have chosen other methods for study. We did not use observational methods. We opted explicitly for linguistic methods. We used language as our analytic tool. David Duncombe commented critically that there was no primary observation of the supervision dyad. That's correct. Margaret Steward lifted up the interesting point that by not observing the dyad, we left an "unmonitored space" which may have been necessary to the progress of the intense dyadic relationship. What risks do we take if we leave observation out? What risks do we take if we insist on having complete observational access?

Let me just mention that our four kinds of linguistic analysis balance one another. The case study is self-report. The adjective check list gathers self-perception material. The metaphor analysis focuses on the use of certain idioms in conversation. The speech act analysis employs structural methods to chart conversation. There are two analyses that focus on the individual and two that focus on conversation.

The third area where questions might be lifted up has to do with the role of language training in professional schooling. I got turned on to Lev Vygotsky during this project. His understanding of "word meaning" and his approach to the study of language in social context became very interesting to me. I am inclined to apply Vygotsky by proposing the notion that "practice" is constituted through concept generation, formation and use. This makes room for a Vygotskian view of language training in mastering concepts which are operational in the delivery of professional services.

A second language issue that we played with is caught up in our concept of "loop." We identified one kind of teaching-learning relationship which is very personal and intense, in the supervision. We built a meta-loop relationship on that which we called consultation. The consultation relationship used language to facilitate a process to keep the intensity of the supervision relationship related to a community of reference and to a tradition.

A final set of questions pertains to the descriptors we used. We attempted to describe the supervision relationship using four principles detailed in the paper. We also attempted to describe the consultant meta-relationship using three principles. We called the seven principles "an hermeneutic." Do they hold together for you? We also wonder about the political fate of our three proposals for professional schooling. My school would have to change rather radically if it were implemented.

Rebecca, do you want to add some things?

Slough: One of the underlying assumptions with all our language analysis is that we believe that meaning is something that is constructed. It is in acquiring meanings of words and concepts together through a relational process that meaning emerges. I think that in much of the way we've conceived of schooling, meaning is something that floats out here that we may snatch occasionally. That's a notion of meaning that David and I did not hold as we went into this project. In our view the supervisory relationships were constructed worlds.

Wuellner: Was that a deliberate decision you made, to hold to that construction view?

D.Steward: Yes. I think a constructionistic view is one of the things that's intriguing to me in part because it is a view in tension with the assumptions of some of our theological colleagues.

Wuellner: It is in some tension not only with some theological colleagues, but also with nine-tenths of university colleagues. Meaning as somehow floating there - well, that's exactly what we have been operating on for a long time; at least since Plato and other substantive philosophers.

Duke: Margaret, would you care to say a word, either picking up on your written comments or responding to David's response? Maybe we should ask him if his section responds directly to your statement, don't you think?

D. Steward: Yes, I can do that.

Duke: I think we should do that, since we do have one of our respondents here.

D. Steward: Good. Dr. Margaret Steward read the paper as a social science researcher and clinician. She affirmed the action science approach of the project and the use of multiple methods of investigation. She set the project in the context of the sparse literature on the study of interpersonal process over time, and expressed appreciation for it.

Dr. Steward noted the tiny sample used and recommended replication to expand our understanding of several aspects of the interpersonal process revealed by the project. These include studies to determine features unique to the chemistry of the supervisor-intern dyad and the disciplinary focus of the consultant. This could be done by looking at the interaction of a person with multiple partners in the same role relationship.

Dr. Steward noticed, as did Dr. Duncombe, that there was no direct sampling of the supervisor-intern interaction. This is clearly an omission of data. Steward makes the intriguing clinical comment that the omission may well have been critically supportive of the development of the supervisory relationship. Unmonitored space for privacy is something people need, and the consultation relationship may have been possible because space was given. Action science, which seeks to study complex interactions and which is overtly interventionist, may pay a price for its scope and honesty.

Of the ideas Steward generates for future research, I would like to underline the study of post-supervision impact. It may be that change derived from concept generation, formation and use requires time to settle into a person as a new version of world, and reveals itself beyond the time of the intervention.

Just one more comment about the character and outcomes of our research: most of Jack Seymour's comments worked out of the assumption that we were engaged in program evaluation in this project. I need to say mea culpa. We did say at two points - and he cites both of them - that we are doing evaluation of a program. That's simply inaccurate. But the question remains: given our interest in exploring interaction, where do we evaluate? In areas like teaching, learning and practice, it's awfully hard to find results within the time frame of the interaction itself. The notion of waiting for program evaluation two years, five years, ten years down the road - as Marge has suggested - is very intriguing. It makes the task of this exploration far more formidable. We can't change our test conditions overnight. We're going to have to take a number of risks in crossing over from how we believe something affected one group, then decide what we want to do with the next group. That may be a difficulty of the character of this research.

M. Steward: I believe that this is a very complex project. There is no single methodology that goes with action research. There's no single way to test it. And, speaking as a social scientist, there's no absolute number of dyads or triads or contact which one would have to sample in order to know when you have enough. I put this kind of research - and I think David and Rebecca do too - in the bucket of research that you use as much to generate ideas as to test hypotheses. In the process of doing this kind of research, you gain new insights, begin to look at things in a slightly different way and then go back into the setting or task of helping folk shape toward ministry with a new kind of vigor and a new perspective. It's research where you begin in the middle and end in the middle. You end in a different middle, but you still need to move on. It's not a clean, laboratory, sterile kind of thing. It's complex and, I think, very exciting.

Duke: Questions for discussion? The floor is open.

Anderson: Maybe we should start with some kind of clarification on this matter of the overstatement of the project.   Let's get it stated so that we can know what is legitimate criticism of the project and what really is irrelevant.

D. Steward: Let me try. Seymour's concern with assumptions uncovers the confusion we have perpetrated in the announcement of the topic of our study. He quite correctly quotes us as promising to determining whether NCSCM "was an effective model of theological eucation." He faults us for not doing this. He would, he says, have been satisfied if we had defined the scope "as a critical exploration of four hermeneutical methods for analyzing a relationship in professional education."
    I acknowledge that we have promised something that we did not deliver - program evaluation. All I can say is that we really never intended to do so. However, I don't think we explore four hermeneutical methods either. We use four methods, each of which is linguistic, to explore a set of teaching and learning relationships in order to generate several principles - what we call an hermeneutic - about supervision and consultation. And we make several proposals from our exploration for theological schooling. That's what I understand that we have attempted to do.

Anderson: Did you talk with your supervisors ahead of time and discuss their ideals of supervision? How did you get such a bad supervisor on one side and such a good one on the other? Did you know you were going to get that?

D.Steward: I'm not prepared to say that one was such a bad one and the other was such a good one. We got different ones, and the difference is striking. I think that the kind of contribution that Supervisor 2 could make is terribly important, and was probably lacking in the experience of the first dyad. It may well be that the intern in the first dyad has now been prepared inadequately to cope with the structures and systems of urban ministry.
    The two supervisors clearly were different. They understood themselves differently, in terms of what they were prepared to do. We got them by the luck of the draw. We had a little grant money. We could sponsor a couple of projects in areas that were of interest to our granting source and to us - areas that were called "marginalized."   Things that happen in those areas are so different from what happens in most suburban church settings that we were delighted to get the settings. The supervisors came with the settings. That's not as random as it may sound, because people who are going to be in those settings are there because they are a certain way. I think the luck of the draw was good for us because we had two supervisors who coped with the chaos of those situations in very, very different ways. Using a bit of seminary jargon, one viewed himself in more prophetic terms; the other in more priestly terms. Both of them were doing effective work where they were, though they would not have passed the time of day had we not brought them together. They're very different on every count.

Anderson: Well, I don't want to monopolize the discussion here, but I think what you are saying is absolutely true, however, the presentation in the paper produces a fairly evident value judgment in favor of Supervisor 1. Almost every time, it seems, Supervisor 2 is doing something wrong, in the judgment of the people who are writing the paper. And what we don't have to work with is the actual practice out there in the streets to tell, regardless of his interaction with Intern 2, whether some thing really good was getting accomplished.

D. Steward: Your point, as I hear it, may be like Jack Seymour's or David Duncombe's that we need to frame our language studies within the scope of observed behavior.

Anderson: I think it would fill out the picture for the reader. I don't know whether you have the time to do that, but it does feel as though we haven't quite enough information.

D. Steward: Let me say a word on the data, because I think part of the sense of bias is in the data. The data from which the descriptions come are contained in three half-hour interviews (for each person) during the last six months of the project. Participants were invited to reflect on what had happened to them in supervision. That was transcribed and we tried to get every important idea they generated into our report.

It's clear that the partners Supervisor/Intern 1 were pleased as punch with one another. They got along really well. It's clear that Supervisor/Intern 2 were in a cat fight all year long. Both were strong persons. An intuition we have is that Intern 2 ended this experience with a tremendous sense of strength about herself out of the experience. There are many things that could have happened to her. She held on to herself, made it through this experience, came out the other side intact - not a small thing to happen. But we know that our result has all of the liabilities and arbitrariness of a case study report.

M. Steward: Observational data can be just as arbitrary, and needs just as much interpretation. You can look and look and look. We've done lots of video research. Video presents an atheoretical flow of behavior. You still have to decide what to look for, how to label it, and what to throw out. You can't possibly code every thing you see. There's an interesting discrepancy sometimes between what people say and what they do - and that may be what you're after - the coherence or discrepancy between what these folk say to interviews, to one another, to themselves, and what they do. Sometimes that's fascinating. But observational data in and of itself is not any easier to handle than language. And it's extraordinarily expensive to collect.

Slough: There's a dissertation out called "The First Five Minutes." It's a videotape of exactly that kind of thing. The authors thought they were going to be able to analyze this half hour videotape. After 1500 pages of transcript and analysis, they got through the first five minutes of the video.

Thandeka: Marge, why did you feel it important to tell us about your experience as a moccasin-maker? What in fact were you commenting on in this report? Are your comments related to what David Duncombe was talking about when he suggest the grammar of science as a way of approaching the wholeness of being, and the way of overcoming the "I?"

M. Steward: It was a profound learning experience for me. One of the things that I reflected on in response to David and Rebecca's research was two quite different experiences I've had, both in teaching and learning. One is the experience of working in a medical school setting, both as a social scientist and as a teacher, where there is a premium on language. The patients usually come in with a verbal complaint. We tell our doctors why we're there. And they write down in words what we tell them. In fact, in any medical chart in our medical school, the very same complaint will be written down by four different sets of people, so that there's multiple verbal coding. Things happen very quickly. There's a premium on speed in medical science and in contemporary high tech medicine. You do things as fast as you can: you make fast diagnoses; you move into treatment as quickly as you can. All that pacing sometimes gets incredibly frightening. I pitted that against my experience of working with an Indian teacher who was making moccasins. I spent a year with her that was a process of learning to slow down.

I had to do things, but not in a product-oriented kind of way. I had to do things slowly. The process was very important. I make a comment in my written response about one of my friends who came mid-way through the year and asked my teacher what it was like to work with a white woman. My teacher said that it wasn't <u>too</u> terrible, but that I continued to talk too much and that I hurry, hurry. My teacher would not only slow me down; she would stop me and make me take something out that I thought was perfectly fine. It was technically accurate, but was done too fast. One of my experiences in all of that - and it continues to be a profound reflection for me - is the experience of doing things slowly and knowing what parts of my learning happen very slowly, as opposed to what happens very quickly. I think that one of the nice things about this study is that David and Rebecca follow two dyads over the whole year. There are some kinds of learnings that take a very long time. One of my guesses is that both of the interns now, almost a year later, would say some things differently than they did even on the last day of supervision. My hunch is that they're still processing both some of their experience in their clinical setting and also their experience in supervision. I can't speak as much to David Duncombe's point around silence.

Thandeka: Because silence was a very large part of your experience?

M. Steward: That was a critical part of my experience.

Thandeka: I wonder if in this way you are critiquing, in a rather negative way, too much talk and too much "hurry, hurry."

M. Steward: David and Rebecca did not observe the supervision, so we don't know what role silence played in the supervision itself.

D. Steward: From the reports we know that there was some praying done, and there was some meditation done in preparation for supervision sessions by Supervisor 1.

M. Steward: I know that the pacing issue and the needing to put everything in words (which I initially did with my Tlingit Indian teacher) had to be unlearned. And it took me a very long time. She frequently told me to hush up and stand behind her. I thought I was being sent into the corner, which really wasn't what she had in mind. She wanted me to stand behind her and look over her shoulder so I could get a different perspective on what was happening.

Luft: It seemed to me that the overall theoretical issue involved in this whole project is the relation between theory and practice in general in our culture. Traditionally that relation has been conceptualized as the priority of theory, with practice reduced to an application of theory. The study was an effort to break out of that and to focus on action. I feel that in a study which is directed against a traditional approach the study is itself defined in that oppositional relationship. What I got out of the examples Marge gave was a nontraditional, non-Western understanding of action which doesn't see it or define it as something in relation to theory but, rather, which conceptualizes action, or thinks about action, or approaches action in a more radically different way than we can understand. For this reason I question the value of understanding action in terms of the Western antithesis between theory and action.

D. Steward: My framing is to locate the action, about which we choose to care, in language. I believe that language is a dominant tool of theory in our culture. Maybe you can help us find out how to study action which is understood to occur within the absence of words. Let me say something personal. Marge and I both are members of the Religious Society of Friends, so silence is not an unknown part of our own practice. We find it very powerful. It is not our notion that silence is the absence of anything. But it's not obvious how to plan, design, teach with that as one's primary tool.

Luft: Actually, I wasn't thinking so much of a dichotomy between silence and language as between language and theory. I don't think that language is necessarily, or needs to be understood as, informed with theory or thought or concepts. Language is an action, and certain kinds of linguistic events generate meaning which is not an "encapsulate intention" but, rather, which defines, or expresses, or creates a meaningful design - even interpersonally in the utterance. I think it's very hard for us to talk about language in that way, because it's so outside of our traditional way of thinking.

Wuellner: We spent a whole colloquium once with John Searle in just that issue of language creating meaning and language as expression of intentional states (see Protocol of the 44th Colloquy of the Center for Hermeneutical Studies with John R. Searle on Meaning, Berkeley, 1982). I wish he were here to pick that up.
    But silence is not understood, is it, as being synonymous with unmonitored space and privacy. In fact, why is that whole privacy issue so important to some of you who commented on it? Is that not a bogus issue? Why should there be privacy in any kind of learning experience which, to me, is always a very social and, as such, a public act?

M. Steward: I do a lot of supervision. I supervise young therapists who are working with very disturbed children and with adults. I think it's hard work. It's also hard to reflect on that hard work. You take a lot of chances, as a student, when you come into a supervisor with as much material as you can present, with your errors, with your fears, with your anxiety. I think had David and Rebecca had a video camera or an audiotape going, that possibly the intern - and even the supervisor - would not have said as much as they needed to say to get their work done. They might have filled some of those silences with words when they shouldn't have. They might have hushed up when they should have said something. They had work to do, and I think to have taken the research inside that dyad by recording it may well have interrupted their work.

When you're using yourself as a tool to reach out in a caring and compassionate way, you don't always do it well, even if you're extremely experienced. To reflect on your work and continue to grow, you need some kind of protection, some kind of private space to do it, I think, that's unmonitored.

Wuellner: One of the issues we might want to discuss some more is the polarity between privacy and public areas as one so pervasive, at least in Western culture.

D. Steward: One of the things that my friend, Jack Seymour, writes about a lot is the notion of the public. His critique, it seems to me, falls right in with his concerns about the public. I think publics require products, results. It's in terms of results that a public is constituted and maintained. It may be that results are less determinative if one is looking at an intense interpersonal dyad. Or maybe results can be more idiosyncratic in that kind of a frame. We may have to talk about results differently within a dyad than we do within a community of reference.

Wuellner: But even silence can be taken as an interactive expression - as a kind of language, too, can't it? It is an interpersonal, interactive thing, as Quakers do when they are in silence: the use of silence can be intensely interactive.

D. Steward: And if you have a community that understands that, it can be dealt with.

Duke: I'd like to press that one point, perhaps on behalf of Jack Seymour, by focusing on another way of getting at it, which is, David, through what is, the "learning" that has occurred in this teaching-learning relational hermeneutic. And if we have an answer to that, you might then be able to tell us what is the "teaching" as well.

D. Steward: You've gone very much to the heart of it. Learning and teaching happen, to begin with, in the supervisory dyad. That dyad is constituted with an experienced practitioner and an intern. What happens in that dyadic relationship is that the experienced practitioner engages in practice directed to the intern. The intern experiences that practice, thereby learning what that practice is about.

Our diagram may help explain. I'm not talking about the content of a discipline. I'm not talking about the skills into which one is trained. Rather, I'm attempting to talk about the action through which what is at the heart of a profession gets out. Let's look at the medical field for an example. Practice is the healing that a physician does - not the cutting and sewing; not the naming of the bones of the body. Or, practice is the act of diagnosing - not the mastery of this or that symptom, but the decision, the judgment that these things have happened and count and are weighted so that treatment can proceed. What is learned is the experience of practice. What is taught is practice, through the activity of practice itself.

Duke: Let me go around again, because I'm still struggling to understand what you mean. What I see is a set - indeed, several sets - of interpretive responses to interaction, a kind of early, middle and late report that has come to you two as evaluators who have tried, in case study format, to analyze what has happened here. Intern 1 and 2 have gone through a personal, indeed an interpersonal process, which they have interpreted in several different ways. They have, so to speak, changed their minds and themselves over the course of this inquiry. Is that the learning?

D. Steward: That's part of the learning. We were required to go beyond the supervision loop. If we limited ourselves to that personal level, it seemed not to come 'round. It seemed to be left hanging. We added a "meta-level" in an effort to clarify and hopefully facilitate the learning of what was personally experienced and what was life-changing in a way that could come to be public with reference to a community and a tradition. We talked about the generation, formation and use of concepts. I can relate intensely with another person (e.g., through a supervision experience) without language. The relation can be enacted with idiosyncratic language, so that my supervisor and I both have some sense of movement or progress. In the final analysis, supervision becomes professionally useful only to the extent that what has happened to me and what I have learned to do is given language that relates my experience to some community of reference.

Duke: Can you illustrate that for me by one of the two interns?

D. Steward: Yes - the experience of Supervisor 1 and Intern 1 which at one point I called "the dark of winter." They had had two or three deaths within their community and they were both extremely stressed. The outcome of that struggle was articulated by the supervisor using the metaphor of wounded healer. He proposed vulnerability, which was something that he was feeling at that time, as an agenda to play out over the Spring. The intern experienced vulnerability that Spring when several of his youth left his program. As a result of the supervision process, he came to be able to approach the youth he felt had rejected him and say "What's wrong? I'm sorry." He learned to open himself up to the youth and act in a vulnerable way. There was a migration from the experience of deep, profound personal and interpersonal distress to the finding of language (the word "vulnerable") first by the supervisor, then by the intern. Each of them could use the word in a way that could be understood and acted on by the other, and in a way that the feedback writer could understand. That movement, I believe, is an illustration of concept generation, formation and use.

Luft: I took your emphasis to be the learning that was going on, to be the learning of a process, or a process of communication and and interaction for a certain purpose in a ministerial function. It seemed to me that the comments of Duncombe were suggesting that perhaps one way to look at what was really happening in that supervision was a process of behavioral training in how to be a professional and how to use language as a professional. He was suggesting that there was a whole other realm of discourse and of action that needed to be responded to, and that was on a street or in a community. It may be that the whole language has to be generated in that context, and perhaps the appropriate word that would come out might not be "vulnerable" - that is, "vulnerable" in a professional context has a certain meaning.

D. Steward: Duncombe suggested that the log structure was not a kind of structure that street people could understand. The language was elitist language. I agree with him that the terminology used between supervisor and intern was elitist. But the process of working linguistically through an experience is a universal process in the human community. If we were to engage the street people in a supervisory conversation, we would have to use different words. Our interns and supervisors live in a relatively ordered world. The people on the streets and the people who work with them are very clear that the sense of time and planfulness on the street is different. Different language use will reflect this.

Luft: I was wondering whether the understanding of process, as a process of going from mindlessness to mindfulness, doesn't itself come out of a professional context. I mean, the assumption is that the communication process or meaningful interaction is somehow universal. I keep thinking of the example of the moccasins - that there are other ways to be with one another - other ways to communicate. I wonder whether we don't carry into the streets, into the community, a model which is still fairly intellectual and fairly elitist.

D. Steward: What we have done represents our history and the history of the supervisors and interns. You are calling me to remember other histories and make a bridge. That's a very substantive part of learning "practice."

Wuellner: I take it you are using "communicative" and "interactive" synonymously, interchangeably. To base a hermeneutic, as you do, with all four models on the linguistic model, may be more of a liability, because all that linguists really care about is communication - the coding, encoding, decoding of communication. But they are not interested in interaction. They may be interested in whether you understood, that is, decoded what was encoded; but they're not interested in learning as interaction.

Slough: John Gumperz (at UC Berkeley) engages in anthropological linguistics. He is one who believes quite strongly that indeed communication is something quite different from interaction. But an interaction occurs as people read meaning using language, or using other things like silence and pauses and other prosodic features.

D. Steward: The assumption we make is that the person is active in dealing with whatever impact the world has on that person. That activity produces a construction through which the things that impact on the person are modified. What we're claiming here as universal is that kind of person-activity. We call the product of that activity "meaning" or "version of world" (to use Nelson Goodman's term). The question of the boundary of language and the bias of language, I think, continues to be important. I don't know how to be active intellectually without some kind of meeting. That may be through words, or it may be through something else.

Luft: Something that occurred to me as I was reading your discussion was a work you didn't refer to because it's in another area but it's very much on the subject: it is Andrew Harrison's Making and Thinking: A Study of Intelligent Activities (Indianapolis: Hackett Pub. Co., 1978). It's subject is practice in the area of art and aesthetics. Harrison distinguishes between purposive activity - that is, actively conditioned by thought or intention - and a different way of designing through action, through the doing. Action painting is one example he uses. The artist doesn't paint what he intends but allows the design to emerge in the course of the painting. It interested me very much as a model of action, of doing and making, which was trying to avoid understanding it somehow as an expression of intention.

D. Steward: It's like the report Edmund Carpenter makes in his book, Eskimo Realities. Carpenter gives a pencil to an Eskimo who has never drawn before and invites the Eskimo to draw a spirit - which is of course a reality that is very dominant to him. When the scribbles come out, the world of that Eskimo has changed. Carpenter's book, Oh, What a Blow the Phantom Gave Me, makes the same point about the power of patterns surfacing through the agency of a human being, where the power is beyond the intentionality of the individual.

M. Steward: One of the things that I forget sometimes when I read your paper is that all of the material that came from the supervisor and from the intern is material which they selected out of their own action, out of their own experience with the world. They selected whatever they jolly well pleased to share with you. You didn't say, "Okay, today you're going to learn how to be a minister. Let me hear all the X, Y, Z things you've done. Tell me about all the praying you've done and all the souls you've saved and all the whatever." You said, "What's up? What have you been doing? What's happening?" And they selected the things that are the content. It would be interesting in another study to see what actions and experiences people decided were appropriate to conceptualize as ministry. You didn't tell them what to write; you just said, "I want it in a format that I can understand, but you can tell me anything that makes sense to you or didn't make sense to you, or that you categorize as having something to do with the practice of ministry." They actively selected what material to raise up.

D. Steward: The metaphor analysis gets at how our people think about ministry.

Slough: Yes. What we tried to do in that analysis, using the interviews and the logs was to figure out ways the talk revealed how our people understood ministry.

M. Steward: Intern 1 was, I think, a clear example.

Slough: Yes. He was the helper, and primarily the communicator-instructor. He was going to tell people this and he was going to teach people this... At the beginning of the group, you could see an instructor notion of ministry. He wrote to us things he is instructing people about or talking to them about. Later in the year that notion of ministry starts to expand. He's not only telling people things; he's also being told things by people. His reports show that this expansion impacts the way he carries out his ministry.

Wuellner: Maybe he has been told before, but this is the first time he notices it.

Slough: Could be.

Wuellner: And maybe, like your first five minutes, you are seeing that same videotape umpteen times and you see new things every time. What would happen if the same interview were rewritten by the same person umpteen times under different circumstances? But you have only one version.

M. Steward: But you are arguing that the guy's doing the same thing the whole time. It sounds to me like Rebecca's saying he's doing something different at the end of the year than he was at the beginning. It's not the same vignette replayed 20 times.

Wuellner: I'm assuming he may be doing exactly the same thing but only begins to notice what earlier he wasn't able to see. Certainly the interview was not able to proceed, because he wouldn't write about the interview.

M. Steward: I would claim he wasn't doing the same thing earlier, if he didn't know he wasn't doing it.

Slough: I would claim that too.

M. Steward: His sense of himself at the two points in time would be really quite different.

Wuellner: But he still may be doing the same thing - that is, in terms of action.

D. Steward: That's right. We analyzed only the report. We didn't observe the behavior.

Leahy: Do his metaphors change?

Slough: Yes, they expand.

M. Steward: At the beginning he kind of had one song, one verse. Later his language showed a more complex perceived relationship.

Leahy: David, I had a question at the beginning and it keeps staying with me. The title says "Teaching and Learning Practice." It doesn't say "Teaching and Learning Ministerial Practice." And it says "A Relational Hermeneutic for Professional Schooling" - not "Professional Theological Schooling" or "Seminary Schooling." However, when examples come up in the paper, they are always concerned not only with ministry but with Christian ministry. Yet the implementation of the title seems to be exclusively in universal terms. Is the main thrust of the paper toward a method of professional schooling - teaching and learning - that is common to all professional schooling? Is that the main concern? Or is the main concern for the ministerial context, the situation out of which the study arises?

D. Steward: My main concern is professional schooling, broadly. The grant we had was funded by somebody who was interested in theological schooling and specifically youth ministry. When we wrote this, we did the best we could in our citation of sources to stretch beyond ministry. The final product, nonetheless, is more narrow than I would like. We had two respondents from medical contexts (Margaret Steward and David Duncombe) because we hoped to generate conversation beyond the seminary. Our project gathered data in an experimental theological school setting. We believe it has pertinence for other professional school settings. One of the sources we've used for our work is Donald Schoen's <u>Educating the Reflective Practitioner</u>. Schoen writes about educating folk to practice music, counseling, architecture and management consultation. His work is being read quite widely in theological school circles now. Nonetheless, the data we drew and the analyses we did were limited to an alternative program of theological schooling. We hope our work will interest and stimulate research by educators in other professions.

<u>Wuellner</u>: Tom, your question brings up the issue so central ever since Schleiermacher, namely whether there should be a separate and special theological-religious hermeneutic, as over against a general secular hermemeutic.

<u>D. Steward</u>: This was an issue that Sara Little raised. She recognized that the process we were working on was not automatically or obviously founded in any community's system of belief. She called us to task for that and said, essentially, if this is going to be useful to us Presbyterians or whoever the "us" is, you've got to take more direct account of the philosophical, theological assumptions that we have.
    If the meta-relationship we have posited in our study is with a community of reference, it's precisely the tradition of that community and its language that must be brought to bear on the teaching-learning relationship. I would claim that the kind of work that we have done here can service any community and any tradition, and I would feel very unhappy letting the normative claims of a given community or tradition define this research.

<u>Wuellner</u>: But there's your old linguistic "red herring" again: claiming to know the basic rules of how language functions, one can then apply them to anything, as long as one has the basic principles straight.

<u>Duke</u>: No, I would think the claim is simply that it would apply wherever practice is the goal - that is to say, where you are dealing with the mid-level of David's diagram. And therefore it would be universal not because of linguistics but because of its own particular normative interest.

<u>Steele</u>: I have one question that I don't know quite how to put, which I think perhaps lies beyond the scope of what you're trying to do, but which in light of the conclusions, I believe is still important. I am tremendously helped by the work you've done. Interestingly, I have served in all three of the roles that you've identified at different times in my life, so it was helpful from a personal perspective to reflect on that. I find myself concerned for the communities themselves in which the ministry is taking place and the fact that they may not see how they are addressed or questioned about the meaning of the learning-teaching ministry that's going on in that context at all. Again, I think that's beyond the scope of what you are trying to do, so that's not in any sense a criticism of the work. I believe, however, in terms of the conclusions about making practice a context for teaching and learning, including the methodology, there has to be some way of engaging those communities in conversations about the meaning of that happening there, particularly if we're talking about communities that have by their very nature been abused. What does it mean to members of the community? What does someone from the community feel has happened both to them and to the intern, the supervisor and the consultant, as a result of that having taken place there?

<u>D. Steward</u>: In many ways, Supervisor 2 was attempting to help Intern 2 know the structure and the language of the street. This is one link between community and educational structure. In addition, there could be experts in street living whose job it is to consult with the dyad that is involved in giving and receiving practice. School faculty can also serve as consultants, when the language system of reference is, for example, theological or ecclesial. There are two or three supervisors in the Network Program who would not be inclined to do what Supervisor 1 did, but who are very street savvy folk. To be in contact

with them gives an opportunity for a special kind of consultative learning - mastery of language and concepts that work on the street. When a seminary student moves into a new and alien territory, like the street, a supportive supervisor, like Supervisor 1, seems pretty important. But that intense interpersonal structure needs to be supported by something that is beyond that relationship - a consultant who represents the community responsible for the practice being learned. This is the dynamic for the teaching and learning of practice that we propose.

PROTOCOL SERIES of the Colloquies:

Protocols not listed are no longer in print. The others are available at $5.00 each;
beginning with the Protocol of the 49th Colloquy, the cost is $6.75 each, (US funds)

...sey Shepherd, et al. *The Commentary Hermeneutically Considered* (11 Dec. 1977)

...rge D. Kilpatrick. *A Textus Receptus Redivivus?* (12 March 1978)

...er R. L. Brown. *The Philosopher and Society in Late Antiquity* (3 December 1978)

...ry Chadwick. *The Role of the Christian Bishop in Ancient Society* (25 February 1979)

...hony A. Long. *Soul and Body in Stoicism* (3 June 1979)

... F. Meyer. *Self-Definition in Early Christianity* (6 January 1980)

...fgang Iser. *Spenser's Arcadia: The Interrelation of Fiction and History* (13 April 1980)

...rie A. Wilson. *Interpretation, Meta-Interpretation and Oedipus Tyrannus* (26 May 1980)

...lio Gabba. *Greek Knowledge of Jews up to Hecataeus of Abdera* (7 December 1980)

...rles Kannengiesser. *Holy Scripture and Hellenistic Hermeneutics in Alexandrian Christology: The Arian Crisis* (6 December 1981)

...ert M. Grant. *The Problem of Miraculous Feedings in the Graeco-Roman World* (14 March 1982)

...dell Clausen. *A Commentary on Virgil's First Eclogue* (6 June 1982)

...n R. Searle. *Meaning* (3 October 1982)

...s Robert Jauss. *The Dialogical and the Dialectical Neveu de Rameau: How Diderot Adopted Socrates and Hegel Adopted Diderot* (27 February 1983)

...mas Conley. *Philon Rhetor: A Study of Rhetoric and Exegesis* (30 October 1983)

...vin A. Judge. *On Judging the Merits of Augustus* (29 April 1984)

...L. Kustas. *Before Discourse* (16 December 1984)

...ven Knapp and Walter Benn Michaels. *Against Theory 2; Sentence Meaning, Hermeneutics* (8 December 1985)

...zabeth Schuessler Fiorenza. *Theological Criteria and Historical Reconstruction: Martha and Mary, Luke 10:38-42* (10 April 1986)

...mas Gelzer. *How to Express Emotions of the Soul, and Operations of the Mind, in a Language that Has No Words for Them; Exemplified by Odysseus and Calypso* (8 February 1987)

...fgang Fikentscher. *Modes of Thought in Law and Justice: A Preliminary Report on a Study in Legal Anthropology* (26 April 1987)

...vid Steward. *Teaching and Learning Practice: A Relational Hermeneutic for Professional Schooling* (13 March 1988)

FORTHCOMING

...rles Kannengeisser. *A Conflict of Christian Hermeneutics in Roman Africa: Tychonius and Augustine* (16 October 1988)

ORDER FORM

...e send _____ of _____ _____ _____
    (copies)   (Colloquy number)

...INSTITUTION _____

...SS _____

_____

Standing Order requested to begin with Colloquy No. _____

Purchase order number _____

date of order _____

BILLING ADDRESS (if different from Delivery Address):

_____

_____

Send _____ of MONOGRAPH 1: *Philo's Rhetoric* at $10 each
   (copies)   plus $2 postage and handling.

...ENTER FOR HERMENEUTICAL
...UDIES in Hellenistic and Modern Culture
...0 RIDGE ROAD ◇ BERKELEY CA 94709

Make checks payable to the *Center for Hermeneutical Studies*